# FREEDOM
## Permits

"even an ignorant ranch hand
from "Flyover Country"
to express his opinions
with no regard to
political correctness"

# Don Stuart

Amazon Publishing

1st Edition 2014

Copyright 2014 Don Stuart. All rights reserved

Cover design by: John M. Christy – JMC graphic design*WORKS*
Text is set in Trajan and Adobe Garamond

ISBN-13: 978-1500966263
ISBN-10: 1500 966266

Amazon Publishing

# TABLE *of* CONTENTS

*This book is dedicated to my wife Darla. She has the patience of a fisherman and loves me like a bulldog puppy.*

# INTRODUCTION

*"I have great confidence in the common sense of mankind in general."*
Thomas Jefferson

First of all, as you will see, I have opened several chapters with a quote from Thomas Jefferson. The reason for that is simple: Thomas Jefferson's words are equally relevant now, as they were 225 years ago. Truth and common sense never go out of style. I am not obsessed with Thomas Jefferson and have no illusions about some of his indiscretions. I believe he is near the top of the list of the greatest American patriots to have walked on American soil. He also had no concept of political correctness. He spoke his mind as truthfully and plainly as he could. In some instances I have multiple Jefferson quotes. I also have several quotes from Ronald Reagan for the same reasons. In the chapters that I failed to find an appropriate Jefferson or Reagan quote, I quoted someone with equal relevance to the chapter content. There are even a couple quotes with my name on them; not because I'm one of the greatest American patriots but simply because what I said was extra relevant to the chapter.

Let's get right to the rat killin'! Throughout the book I will establish myself as a bigot, racist, sexist, homophobe, Islamaphobe, and every other possible "phobe" and derogatory label that can be hung around the neck of a Conservative. I will consider each and every one of these labels to be a badge of honor. The reason I will consider each of these labels to be a badge of honor is because if I upset some people that means I may have brought out an inconvenient truth. Some people consider the truth to be a burden. The truth has no place in the advancement of their ideology/political agenda. I am completely disillusioned with our dysfunctional governmental system and as you'll see very early on in the book I'm not afraid to call out anyone regardless of race, creed or political affiliation.

The cover of the book specifically states that the contents herein are not, and I repeat, not, politically correct. I have not, and will not, fall into the trap called political correctness. My First Amendment right of Freedom of Speech will not be stifled with name-calling. In 1872 Mrs. George Cupples said: "Sticks and stones may break my bones but names will never hurt me". That is exactly the attitude I take throughout this book. You'll also notice that I like quoting other people. It is comforting to know that there are others out there that think the same as I do.

5

The contents of this book will cause you to experience different emotions. You may be totally indifferent about some topics. Some things will surprise you. Some things will anger you. There will be moments when you will be mildly amused and other times you will laugh out loud. Some readers will be insulted. They have a God-given right to be offended and I have a God-given and constitutional right to offend them. Actually, the only people that should be offended are the ones that can't deal with the truth. For those of you who think like me I hope this book is a fun read and an overall enjoyable experience. Using the word "FREEDOM" in the title and the graphics of the American flag both symbolize my pride in America. If you don't like either or you don't enjoy the back cover you probably won't read this book. Speaking of the back cover, I got my inspiration from Clint Eastwood for his thoroughly entertaining and accurate empty chair routine at the Republican National Convention. I would also like to point out that I was not aware of Michelle Malkin's empty chair contest until it was too late to submit mine. It probably would have gotten more attention on her website than it will get on the back cover of my book; that remains to be seen.

If you can't stand the light of truth shown on what you're doing maybe you should stop doing it. Do I claim to be perfect? Absolutely not! Do I claim some fancy moral authority that gives me the right to judge others? Absolutely not! But I do have the right to express my opinion about the public words or actions of others who have put themselves in the limelight. I know if this book is successful my life, lifestyle, and past will be closely scrutinized. I will have put myself into that position to allow the scrutiny by others. Get over it, I will.

I cover a large number of topics; some are several pages and some are very few pages. None of the topics are short because of a lack of information. I just chose not to elaborate on that topic. It is amazing what information is available on the Internet with very brief excursions into its "twilight zone". There are many levels of "truth" on the Internet. If I came across conflicting information I made an effort to confirm which was true. In some cases I actually had to choose what I felt was the most plausible. If I chose wrong in some cases I'm pretty sure I will be adequately chastised! If I did choose wrong I would like to take this time up front to apologize to the reader. Not getting some information accurate will be the only reason I will apologize in reference to this book. I will not, under any circumstances, apologize for the expression or content of any of my personal opinions. All of the opinions in this book are my own; no one else is responsible for, nor can be held accountable for, my ignorance. Over the course of the book keep in mind that these are my opinions; everyone has opinions. The opinions I express in this book are based on facts obtained from other sources. I didn't make anything up. When opinions are involved there are few things more egregious than putting words into someone else's mouth. Accuracy, especially with quotes, is critical. There are times when I paraphrase rather than reproduce a lengthy quote but I made sure not to change the intent of the statement.

I am a true believer in the old adage "laughter is the best medicine". This quote is one of those gray areas that I had to guess at. Do I give credit to Harry Beecher because it is a spinoff of something he said or do I give credit to Readers Digest because they use those specific words as one of their article titles? I guess I just gave credit to both so I should be safe. I sincerely hope you enjoy some of what I consider humorous. I also like to point out hypocrisy, irony, and I am a complete slave to sarcasm. Geez, I think I just made my first racist statement. Oh well, it only gets worse from here.

Believe it or not I do hope to survive the impending criticism of myself and my book was some dignity intact. Speaking of dignity, as I sit here in my underwear dictating to my computer, I sincerely hope my WebCam is off!

As Jackie Gleason would say: *"and awaaaay we go"*.

# WHO'S WHO IN THIS BOOK

**ACORN** – the Association of Community Organizers for Reform Now, was established in 1970 by Gary Delgado and Wade Rathke, both liberal/socialists. Rathke has a direct association with Bill Ayres, Obama's neighborly domestic terrorist. Acorn started out advocating for low income families on several social issues. In 2009 and 2010 they were immersed in several controversies in which their employees were videotaped giving some very questionable advice to individuals posing as clients. There are ongoing investigations into their fraudulent actions. The intensity of the negative publicity forced them to change their name from ACORN to COI, Community Organizations International. But don't be fooled by the name change, they are the same fraudulent voter registration organization that Barack Obama was intensely associated with in the 1990s. Members of COI (ACORN)and similar liberal groups are currently employed in the very well-paid jobs called Health Exchange Navigators to help individuals get registered for Obamacare. It pays to have friends in high places.

**Akin, Todd** – a Republican and former House of Representatives member from Missouri who lost an election for a Senate seat because of the liberals imaginary Republican "war on women".

**Alinsky, Saul** – considered to be the father of our modern "community organizing". His radical socialist views are apparent in America today in forms such as Occupy Wall Street and illegal immigrant amnesty marches. In his book Rules for Radicals, "Rule #4: Ridicule is man's most potent weapon". Rule #4 is currently being successfully used by Barack Obama against Republicans.

**Beecher, Harry** – an evangelical minister and abolitionist activist during the Civil War era. The quote is a spin-off of what Beecher actually said: "Mirth is God's best medicine".

**Branson, Richard** – a multibillionaire British entrepreneur controlling in excess of 400 companies under an aggressive investment group called Virgin Group. He immerses himself in global social engineering but has no qualms about hiding his wealth in offshore accounts and complicated trusts. Virgin Galactic is Branson's suborbital space tourist craft.

**Chomsky, Noam** – came to prominence in the 1960s and 70s in direct opposition to the Vietnam War. Chomsky is anti-authority, a social libertarian and anti-American way-of-life as well as an extremely prolific writer and speaker who opposes American capitalism but also the hard-core authoritarian aspects of socialism. If you looked up the word "anarchist" in the dictionary there would be a picture of Noam next to the word.

**Cicero, Marcus Tullius** – Marcus was born 100 years before Jesus Christ. He was a Roman elitist and philosopher who was renowned for his intellect and an understanding of law. Marcus recognized that Rome had its treasonous "enemies within" 2000 years ago.

**Cupples, Mrs. Geprge** – an author in the Civil War era; the phrase appeared in her publication "Tappy's Chicks" with three words changed from a quote in 1862 in a publication printed by the African Methodist Episcopal Church that stated "sticks and stones will break my bones but words will never harm me".

**Darrow, Clarence** – circa 1857-1938; an American lawyer who was a devout believer in unions and an enthusiastic member of the American Civil liberties Union. Gained notoriety as a criminal defense lawyer.

**Elder, Larry** – resides in Los Angeles as a television personality and radio talk-show host. He is a black American conservative with libertarian leanings, or vice versa.

**Freedman, Mark** – an MBA graduate of Yale University, an inspiring author, and a staunch advocate concerning the successful financial future of baby boomers. He has received many honors and awards as an accomplished entrepreneur and economist.

**French, David** – a graduate of Harvard Law school and has taught at Cornell Law school. He is an accomplished author. He is currently counsel for the American Center for Law and Justice and past counsel for the Alliance Defense Fund. He's a captain in the Army Reserve.

**Hastert, Dennis** – a Republican ex-Speaker of the House of Representatives from Illinois from 1986 to 2007.

**Jefferson, Thomas** – the third President of the United States from 1801 to 1809. His early years of schooling were primarily taught by Christian ministers. He attended the College of William and Mary at age 16. He became a lawyer in 1767. He was a devout reader. As a lifetime scholar and politician he was one of America's Founding Fathers and the principal author of the Declaration of Independence.

**Jones, Van** – a hard-core liberal/socialist/Marxist. As an environmental advocate he was appointed by Obama to a new position called Special Advisor for Green Jobs. He resigned the position after only a few months under heavy political opposition concerning his radical political past.

He has made his living as a best-selling author; member of Boards of Directors of several profit and not-for-profit environmental organizations; and a dedicated liberal speech maker.

**Keyes, Alan** – a black conservative author, radio show host, TV personality and a past diplomat in the US Foreign Service during the Ronald Reagan presidency. He is an outspoken Christian and has no fear of political correctness. He has campaigned several times unsuccessfully for the US presidency and U.S. Senate.

**Koch brothers (Charles and David)** – own Koch Industries employing approximately 50,000 people and showing revenues in excess of $115 billion annually. Family money was made in the evil oil refinery business. The brothers are staunch Christians and supporters of many conservative causes and organizations. They fund cancer research, arts, colleges, and a donation of $25 million to the United Negro College Fund. Their evil ways know no bounds.

**Lamm, Richard** – was Democratic governor of Colorado 1975 to 1987. He grew up as a lumberjack, a stock boy, and a first lieutenant in the United States Army. He settled in Colorado but spent too much time in the Republic of Boulder resulting in him becoming a Democrat. He was an early advocate of abortion. He was a lawyer, a writer, and failed at a couple of attempts for the U.S. Senate and Presidency.

**Lizard Lick Towing** – a reality TV show on truTV featuring the antics of a vehicle towing and recovery crew based in Lizard Lick, Georgia.

**Love, Reggie** – personal assistant to Barack Obama beginning in 2007 and ending in 2011. Reggie was Barack's constant companion and tended to all his personal needs.

**Morrow, Lance** – an accomplished and award-winning essayist for Time Magazine for many years beginning in 1965.

**Mason, George** – another of the American Founding Fathers believed to be the author of the US Bill of Rights. He was a strong advocate for a weak federal government but strong State rights.

**McConnell, Mitch** – Republican Senator from Kentucky since 1984. He has been Minority Leader of the Senate since January 2007. He is an advocate for a balanced-budget amendment and gun rights. He opposed Obamacare.

**Morgan, Piers** – an English journalist transplanted into American liberal television. He replaced Larry King on CNN and lasted for three years.

His downfall began when he took it upon himself to chastise the American population based on their love of guns and their Second Amendment right to have them. CNN removed him from their programming in March 2014.

**Muslim Brotherhood** – the organization has had a rather checkered past as radical supporters of Islam and the Quran. They've been in existence since the late 1920s but have been banned by most Middle Eastern governments. They came back into prominence in Egypt in 2011with the support of the Obama administration but ruled so radically they were deposed by the Egyptian military. They are again banned.

**Nostradamus** – the French version of a modern-day doctor who lived from 1503 to 1566. He is most famous for his collection of historical prophecies. Many believe his prophecies have been extremely accurate over the years. Many others believe that the vagueness of his prophecies has allowed them to be interpreted as any and all see fit.

**Resko, Tony** – a friend, mentor, and business associate of Barack Obama since 1990. He helped the Obamas purchase a large home in Chicago in 2005 that had questionable real estate dealings attached to the sale. He is a convicted felon and is currently serving time in prison for fraud and bribery.

**Ritchie, Anne Isabelle** – an English novelist that lived from 1837 to 1919.

**Roe, Lesa** – she served as the first female director of NASA's Langley Research Center from 2005 to 2014.

**Schwartz, Jack** – a writer for The Times of Israel. He has an inexhaustible list of poignant quotes concerning the Israeli/Palestinian history.

**Sensenbrenner, Jim** – a Republican member of the House of Representatives since 1979 representing Wisconsin. Jim is a leader in the fight against illegal alien amnesty.

**Soetoro, Lolo** – he was the adoptive father of Barack Obama from 1965 through 1980. Lolo moved the family to Muslim-dominated Indonesia in 1966 where Barack obtained knowledge of Islam and the Quran. Barack moved back to Hawaii with his grandparents in 1971.

**Stevenson, Adlai** – (1900 to 1965); served as United States Ambassador to the United Nations; ex-Governor of Illinois.

**Tancredo, Tom** – a Republican ex-House of Representatives member from Colorado. He ran unsuccessfully for the US presidency in 2008 and the Republican nomination for Colorado governor in 2014. Tom is pro-life, anti-illegal immigrant, anti-gay marriage, anti-big government, and an outspoken critic of Islamic terrorism.

**Wallop, Malcolm** – (1933 to 2011); Republican US Senator from Wyoming. Advocate for a strong national defense and smaller federal government.

**Westmoreland, Lynn** – U.S. House of Representatives member from Georgia since 2007. He is no stranger to controversy as an advocate for the display of the 10 Commandments at courthouses and is not easily intimidated by political correctness.

**Varney, Stuart** – born in England but has been in the United States since 1974. He is an economic journalist with Fox News Business Network. He is a strong believer in the American capitalistic system which I believe is why he transitioned away from CNN with their left-leaning, anti-capitalism programming.

# POLITICAL CORRECTNESS

*"The notion of political correctness declares certain topics, certain expressions, even certain gestures, off-limits. What began as a crusade for civility has soured into a cause of conflict and even censorship."*
George Bush

*"There is a national problem with suppressing free speech at high schools and colleges in the name of political correctness, and it disproportionately affects conservative and Christian students and student organizations."*
David French

*"As the push for political correctness increases, common sense decreases in equal proportion."*
Don Stuart, 2014

I consider the term "politically correct" to be the greatest roadblock of all time when it comes to honest and open discussion of any topic regardless of how controversial it may be. Let me give you some examples of how liberals use political correctness to stifle honest debate. A conservative says to a liberal: "Let's find ways to help the black community lessen their single-mother crisis". Since the liberal does not want to lose control of the single-mother vote by actually helping find solutions, the liberal reply is: "You are a racist!" A conservative says to a liberal: "Let's ask some women how we can help them with juggling motherhood and career". Since the liberal does not feel motherhood should be equal to career, the liberal reply is: "You are a sexist!" The conservative says to the liberal: "Can we better protect the American people by giving the CIA and FBI more weapons in the war against extremists and terrorists?" Since the liberal believes we are the extremists and terrorists the liberal reply is: "You are an Islamaphobe!" If you will not or cannot advance the discussion with your ideas then your only recourse is name-calling.

Is there anything more ludicrous than being offended by the name of a sports team? Redskins, Saints, Warriors, Bulls, Seminoles, Bucks, Yankees, Red Sox, Cowboys, Savages, Braves, Padres, Brownies, Indians, Fighting Irish, and the list goes on and on. The name Redskins is more offensive to some white liberals than it is to most American Indians. Should atheists be offended by the names Saints and Padres? Should the fighting Irish mascot be offensive to pacifists? Should the names Bulls and Bucks be offensive to heifers and does? I have to assume that Southerners must be offended by the name Yankees!

What is offensive is the fake outrage exhibited by some of the offended. If it is that offensive the solution is simple: don't put yourself in a position that will cause the offense. If you see a sign that has the offensive words on it look away; don't go to the games; don't read the sports page in your favorite birdcage liner; refrain from talking sports with your brother-in-law; stop going to the sports bars; change the channel on the TV and watch a less offensively-named team. Some of these mascot names have been around in excess of 100 years, why suddenly are the names so offensive? Has society changed so much in the recent past that we actually enjoy being offended or do we enjoy the status of victimhood? Life is too short and too precious to waste time on such matters.

There is a never ending outrage about the Washington Redskins football team owner refusing to drop the name Redskins. I hope the owner can hold up to the relentless barrage of idiocy aimed at him. They were originally the Boston Redskins beginning in 1932 and became the Washington Redskins in 1937. There wasn't much controversy about the name until 2004, 72 years after their original naming. It used to take a long time to offend a liberal but not any longer. As Hillary would say: "at this point what difference does it make?" Don't let the word get out, but I would agree with Hillary on this one.

The political left has advanced political correctness to a fine art. They have managed to keep the political right from discussing any of their liberal ideological failings simply by stifling discussion with name-calling. I honestly believe that even the liberals were surprised how easy and effective that would be in silencing their politically-weak opponents.

# AMERICAN EXCEPTIONALISM

*"We will always remember. We will always be proud. We will always be prepared, so we will always be free."* Ronald Reagan

I'm not going to spend a lot of time on this topic even though I believe in it wholeheartedly. Regardless of what the critics of the United States say, there is no better country in the world than the United States of America. The United States has done more to help the world in its short 225 years than the rest of the world has done on its own combined. The United States saved the world from fascism and bondage, not once, but twice. Had it not been for the United States of America stepping in to help out during World War II, half of the world would have been speaking German and the other half would have been speaking Japanese. Had it not been for the United States after World War II all of Europe would have been speaking Russian. Had it not been for the United States and Ronald Reagan all the world would be speaking Russian. To this day, I have never heard a foreigner say "thank you". Americans give more aid of every type including cash, food, technologies, medical, military, etc. than the rest of the world combined. Most of the countries of the world hate America but America is the first country their hand goes out to when they are in need. The entire world knows America can't say "no". They take advantage of our generosity and spit in our faces. If all of this sounds arrogant, so be it. If you can't see how exceptional America is, there's something wrong with the inner workings of your brain. I am sad for those who dedicate their lives in the pursuit of the destruction of America. American patriotism is a much more pleasant experience.

Hard-core liberals like Sean Penn, Danny Glover, Louis Farrakhan, Barack and Michelle Obama, Hillary Clinton, New York City Mayor DeBlasio, and many others, have lived their lives with the attitude that the United States has not earned its status in the world. They feel the US has achieved that status on the backs of others and the rape of the earth itself (their words, not mine). Mr. Obama's comment about "someone else did it for you" was not directed at American businessmen specifically, it was an indictment of America in general. Michelle Obama said, in her lifetime, she was never proud of America until it elected her husband president. Michelle came from a middle-class family; she never had to "get down with the struggle". I'm not sure why living the American dream was such a burden for her. It is very difficult for me to believe that self-anointed liberal critical thinkers could believe that dictators like Cuba's Fidel Castro and Venezuela's Hugo Chavez were good for their respective countries. You have to have some type of mental block not to see the ruthless and deadly ways thugs like that mistreat their citizenry.

I've always wondered why America haters, foreign and domestic, want to come here or stay here if being in the United States is so repulsive to them. I believe, as an American, if I felt that strongly I could easily give up my American citizenship and move to whatever Third World country I consider to be a better place to live. If I already lived in a Third World country, I believe I would be looking for a place other than the US. How can you be repulsed and attracted to something at the same time? There are always a few liberals that swear they will give up their citizenship and leave the United States forever if a Republican is elected president. They were lying. They never leave. In 2016 when we elect a Republican president, don't let the door hit you in the butt on the way out. And don't think for a minute we won't change the locks on the door after you leave.

In closing, I'm going to have a Michelle Obama moment. In my lifetime I have been disappointed in America on four occasions: 1.the treatment of our vets coming home from Vietnam; 2. the music during the 80s; 3. Re-electing Mr. Obama; 4. the treatment of our vets coming home from the Middle East.

# PATRIOTISM

*"Patriotism is not a short and frenzied outburst of emotion but the tranquil and steady dedication of a lifetime."*　　　　　　　　Adlai Stevenson

*"Excellence does not begin in Washington."*　　　　　　Ronald Reagan

*"Patriotism is supporting your country all the time, and your government when it deserves it."*　　　　　　　　　　　　　　Mark Twain

Loosely defined, patriotism is the love of, the defense of, the support of, and the loyalty to one's own nation. With few exceptions the most patriotic Americans throughout the course of history have been our military. They obviously love, support, and are loyal to America because they are prepared to give their lives in its defense. Short of foreign invasion or internal revolution, few Americans will ever have the opportunity to defend America with their lives. I truly hope we never have to find out which Americans are up to the task. There is no way to determine the number of non-patriotic Americans but I can assure you that number would be considerably smaller if America was invaded. Even the gun haters would pick up a weapon in defense of themselves, their families, and their way of life. It would be a shallow form of patriotism but self-preservation has a tendency to turn pacifists into warriors.

Military service may be at the top of the list but it is not the only form of patriotism. The teacher is a patriot if he/she bucks the liberal school system and still leads the class in the Pledge of Allegiance each morning. You are a patriot when you pick up an American flag from the sidewalk of a liberal college campus when it is being used by students and faculty to wipe their feet. You're a patriot when you defend America from the haters. You're a patriot when you fly the flag at your house or business even if you fly it only on the appropriate holidays. You are a patriot when you do a kindness for an active service member or veteran even if all you do is say "thank you for your service". You are a patriot if you believe in American "exceptionalism". You are a patriot if you are loyal to America regardless of her past indiscretions. You are a patriot if you honor the Constitution of the United States as written.

Patriotism can be a state of mind that is as easily lost as it was to learn. If it comes from the heart it is not so easily shaken. You feel sadness when you witness a military coffin coming off a plane, but at the same time there is an extreme sense of pride for that fallen hero and his/her family. To realize that hero gave his/her life in a far-off land in defense of you and your family is very humbling. That is the ultimate patriotic gesture.

Everyone is allowed to pick and choose who they consider to be American patriots. I believe there are fewer "dyed-in-the-wool" patriots in the federal bureaucracy in Washington than you might expect. There are many in Washington that do not love America, have no specific loyalty to America, and do not support or defend America. They all claim to be patriots but as everyone knows: "actions speak louder than words". I don't have to name non-patriots because everyone, including them, knows who I am talking about. What I am going to do is name some Americans who I consider to be patriotic beyond reproach: Representative Louie Gohmert (R - TX); Senator Mike Lee (R-UT); Senator Ted Cruz (R-TX); Representative Michele Bachmann (R-MN); Ben Carson, retired neurosurgeon; former Gov. of Alaska Sarah Palin (R); Lt. Col. (Ret) Oliver North (R); former Representative (R-FL)Lt. Col. (Ret) Allen West; 2012 presidential nominee candidate Herman Cain (R); Lt. Col. (Ret) Ralph Peters (R);  Representative Trey Gowdy (R-SC); and to prove that patriotism can come in small packages: Conservative author Michelle Malkin. If I were president I would love to have that group available for cabinet selections. That would be the ultimate "Dream Team".

I consider an American who can fend for himself and his family during a crisis a patriot. He has made preparations and is not consuming scarce vital goods that may be needed for the less fortunate. He is in charge of the defense of his person and family and property. The providing of food, shelter, and safety cannot and should not be left up to someone else, and especially not the government. People make fun of "preppers" but those very people will be the first to knock down a prepper's door to steal his provisions. There are different levels of preparation for the calamity whether man-made or natural. But when the calamity hits, and rest assured it will, you are an idiot if you didn't set aside enough essentials to last at least two weeks, more if you can. I will not, for safety reasons, go into any detail about what my household preparations are; just be aware that I am fully prepared and adequately capable of protecting my family and property.

# FREEDOM *of* SPEECH *and* RELIGION

*"The liberty of speaking and writing guards our other liberties."*

Thomas Jefferson

The First Amendment to the Constitution guaranteeing Freedom of Speech is one of the most important of the amendments. The Framers of the Constitution must have felt that way also for it to be the First Amendment. They lived their lives having King George ignore their pleas for representation. They understood how extremely important it was to have a say in how they were governed. King George was taxing every commodity consumed in the New World and to the extent it was unsustainable for the taxpayers. Is this déjà vu all over again? With no right to voice their concerns they were left with no choice but citizen revolt. Fortunately, owning guns allowed them the option of military revolution. Now this story is really starting to sound familiar. Where have I heard of this scenario playing out? Never mind, I'll think of it later. But as history shows, King George ignored the pleas of the New World Americans at his own peril. George spent a considerable amount of his country's treasury and a considerable number of his British countrymen's lives to put down the revolution, but the Americans were determined to wrestle control of their lives from the tyrannical government despot. George's minions were sent packing with their tails tucked between their legs. Now, I'm not kidding, I'm getting this really eerie feeling in the back of my mind. I'm concerned that this exact situation is happening somewhere and has the potential to explode into action. Anyway, it seems George asked for it. You can't keep your boot on the neck of a strong person unless he allows it. When that person gets tired of it there will be consequences.

The McCain/Feingold Campaign Finance Reform is a major encroachment on the First Amendment. Outside the Washington Beltway it is called the "Incumbent Protection Act". CFR disallows anyone being critical of the candidates or discussing their past voting record for the last 60 days prior to an election. Does that not sound like incumbent protection? I think the most important criteria to help determine who to vote for would be the candidate's voting records. If you don't like the way they vote on issues that affect you, you don't want to vote for them. Hiding that information is a disservice, or as liberals call it, disenfranchising the voter. Mr. McCain should be ashamed of himself for co-sponsoring this legislation. This plus amnesty for illegals and a couple other things are what got Mr. McCain on my RINO list.

The policy called the "Fairness Doctrine" is also a major encroachment on freedom of speech. It was designed by liberals to require conservative TV programs and radio talk shows to give equal time to liberal causes as was allotted to conservative programming. I can assure you no attempt to enforce that doctrine on liberal TV and radio would have been attempted. This policy would not be necessary if people would voluntarily listen to liberal garbage on liberal stations. It was designed to mitigate the damage done to liberals by exposing the truth about the detrimental effects of liberal ideology. President Reagan had the good sense to end that policy before it got a good foothold. There is a new form of fairness doctrine that the liberals at the Federal Communications Corporation tried to sneak in under the radar but a conservative member of the FCC board squealed on them. The idea was for the FCC to implement a program of monitoring television and radio news outlets to ensure the public only got news and info that the federal government deemed necessary for the public to have. This new policy would have been called the "Obama Protection Act". The program would require an FCC official to be on location at each station to approve or disapprove information before it was released to the public. Can you say: "comrade news monitor"? Does anyone actually wonder why the American public distrusts their own representative government? When the program was outed, the FCC officials had no choice but to make up lies for the reasons of implementation of the program but under pressure were forced to put the program on hold. And I stress the word "hold" because it will be revived at some point. Mr. Obama has nearly 2-1/2 years left as president; he may very well reinstitute it in some form, probably by another of his executive orders.

Another part of the First Amendment relates to the freedom of religion. The amendment allows Americans to freely practice their religion with no interference from the government. I think this was also of equal importance to the Founding Fathers because the Church of England tried to maintain so much control over the way Americans worshiped. The Church of England had an unholy grip on the governance of England and if you did not adhere to their doctrines your life could be very miserable and very short. Americans wanted the freedom to worship as they pleased or not worship at all. Contrary to what some believe today the Founding Fathers and most all Americans in those days were devout Christians. The First Amendment guarantees Americans the freedom of religion not the freedom from religion. But the Founding Fathers did not count on the atheist crowd being so vocal. I think they made the assumption that if you did not want to worship you didn't have to but they weren't expecting the atheists to try to stop everyone else from doing so. Maybe the atheists are so vocal and disruptive because their feelings were hurt by the Founding Fathers not specifically including them in a constitutional amendment. Get over it. Nowhere in the amendment does it state any such thing as "the separation of church and state". What the amendment states is that the government cannot establish a religion like the Church of England. Putting a stone, with an inscription of the Ten Commandments, on the lawn of an American courthouse does not constitute establishing a religion. I am tired of the American Civil Liberals Union saying so. By the way, did you know the American taxpayers pay the ACLU to sue the American taxpayers? Pretty good work if you can get it!

# MILITARY

*"No arsenal or no weapon in the arsenals of the world is so formidable as the will and moral courage of free men and women. It is a weapon our adversaries in today's world do not have."*       Ronald Reagan

Let me make some quick statements here in the hopes I can save my bashers a little research time. Several members of my extended family served in the military. I did not serve in the military. Every man my age will understand what I am about to say. Drafting for the Vietnam War was in full swing. Many people (liberals) thought that poor and minority boys were being drafted at a higher rate than "privileged" white kids. In order to appease that protest group President Nixon and his administration introduced a draft policy called the "lottery". A drawing was held using all 366 birthdates. The order in which the birthdates were drawn was the order in which individuals born on those dates were drafted. My birth date was drawn beyond 200 giving me little chance of being drafted. With that in mind I went to college. Both of my older brothers served in Vietnam in the late 60s. I'm extremely proud of them and their military brothers and sisters. I am extremely disappointed in America for the way they were treated when they returned from overseas. What made that situation worse was the fact that they answered the call of duty through the draft and not as "gung- ho" volunteers that many portrayed them to be. They were not the baby killers and terrorists that John Kerry made them out to be in front of Congress in 1971.

The American military is the best trained and equipped military on the face of the planet. They are trained and equipped to kill people and break things. We do not need a feel-good, social military. Keep the politics out of military command decisions. If the politicians are so concerned about collateral damage they should not send American troops to battle. Stuff happens in the heat of the battle when bullets are flying and bombs are exploding. You cannot limit our troop's mission by tying a hand behind their backs. When that is done they transition from the best fighting men/women on earth to "cannon fodder". Do not limit the scope of their abilities because you will see an increase in the number of American coffins coming off of planes. The other thing that should never happen to our American troops is to be put under the command of foreign leaders. Those foreign leaders do not have our soldier's best interests in mind when they plan missions. I am talking specifically about the United Nations and NATO.

Another pet peeve of mine has to do with the funding of the US military. The American soldier has long been the liberal whipping boy. An American soldier is notoriously underpaid for the service that soldier provides. Send him halfway around the world to be shot at and throw him a few extra dollars for combat duty. The federal government sends our heroes all around the world to do police actions and crowd control for dictators; that same government treats them badly when they come home. The current administration is making cutbacks that will reduce or eliminate large portions of the medical care and rehabilitation our soldiers require. Their current pay and future benefits are being cut. These are the men and women who put their lives on the line at the request of the Washington politicians and the politicians treat them like second-class citizens. That is disgraceful! Mr. Politician, if you're not going to take care of them then stop sending them in harm's way.

One of the most disgusting scandals to ever come out about the American military is the treatment of our wounded soldiers by the Veterans Administration. I understand that they must work within a specific budget and that the fighting forces must be well-equipped. That does not excuse the behavior of presidential administrations that ignore our wounded heroes. But let's not leave out the executives within the VA itself. The top brass at the VA just got $400 million in bonuses. Civil servants should not get bonuses. They don't produce anything! They claimed that the executives receiving bonuses reached the level of accomplishment that allowed the bonuses to kick in. Given the fact that the waiting lists that have been revealed have probably saved money, should I assume that their level of achievement was attained by the number of wounded heroes not served or by the amount of money saved by not serving them? I don't consider that being rewarded for a job well done but being rewarded for colossal failure that literally cost some veterans their lives. Mr. Obama, please straighten this out like you promised you would while campaigning. Neither of us wore a military uniform but that doesn't absolve us from the duty to properly care for those who did.

When my wife and I travel and we see active military personnel in uniform and veterans (the ones that wear hats are easy to spot), we make a special point to thank them for their service. That small gesture of appreciation should be standard practice by all Americans. You don't have to make a big deal out of it. Just shake their hands and say "thank you".

# GUN RIGHTS

*"The beauty of the second amendment is that it will not be needed until they try to take it."*
Thomas Jefferson

*"The strongest reason for the people to retain the right to bear arms is, as a last resort, to protect themselves against tyranny in government."*
Thomas Jefferson

*"Laws that forbid the carrying of arms...disarm only those who are neither inclined nor determined to commit crimes...such laws make things worse for the assaulted and better for the assailants; they serve rather to encourage than to prevent homicides, for an unarmed man may be attacked with greater confidence than an armed man."*
Thomas Jefferson

A 200 year old truth does not become false with the passage of time!

The Second Amendment of the United States Constitution grants the right of American citizens to keep and bear arms. It does not grant authority to any government entity to infringe on that right. No entity has the right to limit the possession, the sale, the type, the size, the availability, or the use of American guns. No entity has the right under the Constitution to require American guns to be registered or a database of owners to be kept for any purpose. No entity has the right to say if you want to live in a specific geographical area you can't own a gun. A country that has a large population of gun owners is the country that is least likely to be ruled by a tyrannical government either from outside or within its own borders. The very first thing a socialist or communist dictator does is confiscate all guns from the citizens. Once that happens there is no going back. There's no effective form of citizen resistance when there are no weapons to resist with. The citizenry must submit to whatever level of brutality and deprivation they are presented with or they will die. That scenario has played out hundreds of times over the course of man's history, and is still being played out around the world at present. The United States of America is one of the last bastions of personal freedom anywhere in the world and the reason for that is the right of its citizens to have guns. Once the federal government has successfully disarmed the American people there will be no limit to their power and no accountability for their actions. Considering all the damage that the federal government has done with their confiscatory taxes; their suffocating rules and regulations on private land use; drawn out permitting processes; fines and penalties processes; the overall eagerness of all federal agencies to say "no" to us, and back it up with an armed SWAT team, regardless of the questions we ask them or the requests we make of them; it is a wonder we still possess any freedoms at all. I honestly believe that the only thing that prevents the federal government from taking complete control of our lives is the fact that in their minds they know the American citizens will only be pushed so much before we push back. It has been 240 years since that last happened, but history has been known to repeat itself and they know it. They have been acting like King George for a very long time and treating the American citizenry like the New World settlers. We all know how it turned out when King George pushed too hard. I am not advocating violence against the United States government. There is a lot of talking and yelling and civil disobedience that needs to happen before any physical action takes place. I'm 63 years old, I won't live to see the revolution. The Revolution will happen when our great-grandchildren receive the bill we left them from China.

Speaking of King George and the British, what do you think possessed Piers Morgan of CNN to assume he had the moral authority to lecture Americans about guns? His own country has a longer history of gun violence and wars and worldwide occupations than America. Does he feel superior because his country no longer allows citizens to have guns? Each to his own; Americans have a love of guns dating back to the early 1600s when the first settlers landed in New England. Guns have long been the means to protect and feed a family. Over the 400+ years of America's existence guns have saved more lives than they have taken. No, I do not have a statistic or a fancy study to prove that statement. To this day there is no statistic that indicates how many lives were saved from bad guys and countries that walked away because they had a gun pointed at them. I can assure you it would be an extremely large number. As for Piers Morgan, he is off the air at CNN. I never did hear a reason for his removal but I would assume he caused CNN so much backlash and grief they had no choice but to get rid of him. Piers was whining that America turned against him and he didn't understand why, go figure! He will resurface in an even more liberal setting somewhere else. Being an idiot seems to be a resume enhancement to liberals. We kicked the British out of the United States twice and have no problem doing it a third time. The British people are important allies to the United States but guys like Piers Morgan and King George give them all a bad name in America.

The first Fort Hood shooting was a prime example of taking away the good guys guns leaving only the bad guys with guns. The base policy at that time banned anyone from carrying weapons unless they were gate guards, on-duty MPs, or local law enforcement. American military bases house the most professionally trained weapons people in the world. Why would they be banned from carrying weapons on a military base? Seems like bad policy to me. Now we have had a second shooting at Fort Hood. It turns out the weapons ban in place resulting in the first shooting remained in place for the second shooting. It went from bad policy to asinine policy. There are a lot of very smart people in the American military but some security guru, probably a civilian politician, dropped the ball big time. There was no excuse for the second shooting. By the way, the shooter wasn't brought down by a gate guard or an MP. He shot himself when confronted by an armed, female law enforcement officer. That pretty much destroys the argument that the mere presence of a firearm can't stop firearm violence. Don't tell me he would have gone on that base and started shooting if he knew that any or every soldier on base may be packing heat. Mass murderers may be crazy but that doesn't necessarily mean they are stupid. They will go and do their dirty work where there are no guns.

There is a common sense solution that could very well stop the next military base shooting. Establish a 24/7 duty roster of armed soldiers that are on duty at each building on the base. The protection of other soldiers and civilian personnel is that soldier's only duty. If he has to leave the building for any reason he would be replaced by another armed soldier. There is absolutely no reason to allow another shooting on a military base in America. I understand how it can happen on an overseas active combat base, but not at a base on American soil.

I would like to mention a situation that took place in New Orleans beginning immediately after Hurricane Katrina. A local law enforcement official decided the best way to prevent looting was to take the guns away the law-abiding citizens so they couldn't protect themselves from the looters. I am confused by that logic. The only people that were protected by the removal of guns from the citizens were the criminals that would've been confronted by them. I won't mention the name or position of the law enforcement official that hatched that dangerous and unconstitutional policy. Suffice it to say if he is so paranoid about law-abiding citizens having guns to protect themselves with, he should be banned from law enforcement for the rest of his life for his failure to serve and protect. He might even need to be prosecuted for the illegal acts he committed. The last I heard the residents never received their guns back. On the other side of the coin the police chief of the city of Detroit held a press conference and announced to the residents of the city that his officers were no longer capable of keeping the residents safe and their best course of action would be to arm themselves. I believe that man should hold a higher office and be given more responsibilities. Common sense is not a typical big-city attribute when it comes to the right of citizens to have guns; congratulations to the police chief of Detroit for pushing back against its liberal leadership in an effort to protect the citizens.

It has long been a dream of the liberals to confiscate your weapons and make you a prison inmate if you don't turn them all in for destruction. That is exactly what happened in Canada and Australia. Those are examples of what happens to gun ownership when enough liberals congregate in urban areas to control a liberal voting base. They can overrule the gun owners in the mountains and the outback. That is also the scenario that takes place in America's large liberally controlled cities such as Washington DC, New York City, Chicago, and Detroit. The super tough gun bans in those cities have resulted in the highest crime rates in the United States. The liberals on the front range of Colorado voted to ban specific guns and accessories. But there's hope; the law-abiding gun owners fought back. The legislation passed but the gun owners successfully recalled the two top liberals that pushed the ban and caused a third to resign her office to prevent the stigma of recall. I was extremely proud of my home state residents for their ability to rally to such an important cause. It just may give pause to other liberals who are considering the same ridiculous legislation. Michael Bloomberg, who was the mayor of New York City at the time this all took place, put up millions from his personal fortune in the pursuit of the original legislation and also put up funds to protect the liberals facing recall. I sincerely hope Mr. Bloomberg continues to waste his money on similar lost causes.

Well, there went the theory that if you remove guns from society there will be no more mass killings. I don't mean to be flip, but the 16-year-old in Pennsylvania didn't get the memo. He killed several people with a knife. The gun is not the problem and never has been. The problem is the mentally challenged person who decides to go out and kill several other people for whatever demented reason his diseased brain conjures up. A gun on its own has never been responsible for shooting anyone. The responsibility lies with the person who picks up the gun. Without a sick person and his/her intent there is no killing regardless of the weapon. Without a shooter the gun will lay there and disintegrate into a pile of rust. Address the real reason for shootings: the shooters. In a liberal's backwards way of thinking the shooter is the victim and the inanimate object, the gun, is the perpetrator.

The same holds true with liberals when it comes to gas guzzling vehicles. The driver is never responsible for the accident, the driver is a victim and the inanimate object, the SUV, is the perpetrator. Another big roadblock for the liberals in preventing unstable people from possessing guns is the fact that liberals hate profiling. How in the world are they going to be able to determine who the future shooters will be?

If you want to do a little research on mass shootings going back many years you will find that the bulk of the mass shooters were left-leaning kooks. Funny how history continues to repeat itself; liberals continue to try to hang the shootings on evil, gun toting right-wing nuts. It is never successful but not for a lack of trying on their part. Most gun owners are God-fearing, American flag-waving, law-abiding, Mom and apple pie loving individuals that consider gun ownership a constitutional right and a patriotic duty. They take the responsibility of gun ownership seriously. Don't mess with America's guns and don't mess with an American holding a gun!

Mr. Obama's administration has been working very diligently and very closely with the United Nations in an effort to destroy the sovereign right of an American citizen to possess guns. The United States Constitution specifically places the ability to make such treaties with foreign entities solidly in the hands of Congress. The American Congress has successfully thwarted Mr. Obama's efforts to this point. If you consider Mr. Obama's track record with his executive orders it is only a matter of time before he circumvents Congress again and signs some form of illegal agreement with the UN that will effectively take guns away from Americans. This is another treasonable act by Mr. Obama that flies in the face of his oath to protect the Constitution.

# POLITICAL AFFILIATIONS

I'm going to do my own definitions of political groups in the order I consider to be from good to bad.

1. **Conservative:** constitutionally astute; financially and socially productive; Christians with a working knowledge of morality and justice; fiercely patriotic; true believers in American Exceptionalism and capitalism; it is not an insult to them when they are accused of wanting to hold on to their God, their guns, and their American way of life.

2. **Mainstream Or Establishment Republican:** Have a conservative core but tend to be swayed by some liberal social issues; still patriotic but conservative-lite.

3. **RINO** (Republicans In Name Only): still have some conservative core beliefs; tend to blow with the Washington breeze; would rather have friends across the political aisle than advance a Conservative ideology.

4. **Libertarian:** have many conservative-leaning beliefs but have an equal number of liberal-leaning social beliefs; have a bad habit of siphoning off some RINO votes; seem to be a hybrid cross between Republican and Democrat.

5. **Independents:** the voting bloc that everyone courts; wishy-washy voters; hard to nail down and never dependable voters.

6. **Reagan Democrats:** financially responsible but still solidly liberal when it comes to social issues; Libertarian-lite.

7. **Mainstream Democrats:** financially and socially liberal; can be swayed to vote against the grain if it affects them personally.

8. **Liberals:** controlled entirely by emotion; financially and socially irresponsible; zero belief in American Exceptionalism; methods used for advancement of their socialist ideology have no boundaries; "truth, justice, and the American way" truly remain a comic book concept to them.

9. **Socialist:** liberals on steroids; power-hungry government elites that must control all aspects of the lives of the lower class; there is no middle class; all facets of life favor the collective and there's no room in a socialist society for individualism.

10. **Communist: socialists on steroids;** leaders at this level have become so addicted to power and control that the lives of the lower class are no longer relevant; there is no compassion for the huddled masses; toe the party line or die at the hands of the Masters; toe the line, obey the Masters, and die of starvation and disease.

I certainly hope I offended number #2 through #10; the truth seems to have a tendency to do that to some people.

# CONSERVATIVES *vs.* LIBERALS

*"Republicans believe every day is the 4th of July, but the Democrats believe every day is April 15."*                    Ronald Reagan

*"The trouble with our liberal friends is not that they're ignorant; it's just that they know so much that isn't so."*                    Ronald Reagan

*"The art of governing consists simply of being honest, exercising common sense, following principle, and doing what is right and just."*

Thomas Jefferson

*"Socialism is a philosophy of failure, the creed of ignorance, and the gospel of envy; its inherent virtue is the equal sharing of misery."*

Winston Churchill


I'm paraphrasing Great Britain's Prime Minister Margaret Thatcher when in 1976 she said in effect: "The problem with socialism is that eventually you run out of other people's money".

I thought it appropriate to use quotes from two of Great Britain's greatest Prime Minister's in order to make the point about socialism. That country, as well as most of the rest of Europe, has lived with some form of socialism, fascism, or communism for many centuries. They have lived with the lies of socialism but we have not learned from their mistakes.

"A Republican bureaucrat spends his entire political career reacting to liberal actions; seemingly unaware or uncaring that he is watching the slow but methodical implementation of a socialist ideology." Don Stuart, 2014.

If you doubt my statement, tell me one policy or law or directive currently being enforced by the federal government that is friendly to, or initiated by, American Conservatism.

A supposed Chinese proverb has been, over the years, co-mingled with a proverb written by Anne Isabella Ritchie in 1885. Over the years it has been revised even further by adding liberal and conservative to show a clear and undeniable comparison between the two. That version goes like this: "a liberal gives a man a fish and he eats for a day; a Conservative teaches a man to fish and he eats for a lifetime". The ironic part about that is the fact that the liberal has to step in and take fish from the conservative fisherman in order to feed his constituents each day. That is a simple, yet truthful, indictment of liberal ideology.

The most important thing to understand about Conservatives is that their ideologies are derived from thoughts and actions that are based on truth and morals. If, at every level of your life, you do the moral things, keep your nose to the grindstone, and mind your own business, you will find that life in America can be very rewarding. You don't need to be a churchgoing Christian to believe that adhering to the concepts of the 10 Commandments would make for a very satisfying life. If it will make you more comfortable, call them man's laws rather than God's. It won't have the same meaning but would hopefully have the same positive results on society. I do believe that faith will make your life even more pleasant. On the other side of the coin, liberal ideologies are based entirely on emotions and the premise that "If it feels good, do it!" Have you ever noticed how everything the liberal/socialists do is for the kids, or the many minorities, or females, or the poor, and yet everything they do hurts those groups first and the very most?

Liberals believe that all rights are derived from man and thus all rights can be given or taken away at a whim. Adults are no different than children when it comes to the need for consistency, accountability, and stability. A society cannot survive when the laws of man are left to blow in the breeze. The laws must be based on a solid footing and the United States Constitution was intended to be that footing. Liberals have little regard for the United States Constitution. As a "living document" it can be adjusted or tweaked to reflect man's evolving sensibilities for a variety of situations or circumstances. Liberals will go to any extent to bash the Constitution, even trying to adhere to European laws in the hopes they can override ours. I don't know about the rest of you, but I don't want America to be Europe.

From the beginning of our Republic, Conservatives and liberals have fought the battle for the hearts and minds of the American voters. Liberals have won the hearts of the American people by shaming them into believing that every class of people, regardless of race, sex, national origin, or sexual orientation, is a victim of American society. They have pulled on the emotional heartstrings of American people to the point where a good portion of society is heartless. Conservatives, on the other hand, appeal to the intelligence of the American people in the hopes that they continue to possess the self-respect and common sense necessary to keep the liberal/socialist advance in check. That has proven difficult to do with the liberals having had nearly complete success in destroying the American economy and being able to blame it on Conservatives. With the economy in shambles, it makes it even harder when the liberals are portrayed as the proverbial "Santa Claus", eager to hand out goodies. In my world that's called "vote buying".

Conservatives have a tendency to "eat their own" when anything even smacks of impropriety or misconduct because of the conservative moral base. Liberals, on the other hand, go about business as usual regardless of the antics of their members because they don't have a moral base. Bill Clinton is a prime example of the lack of morals that extends right up to the very top leader of their party. The liberals, including and especially Hillary, covered for Bill through all of what Hillary called the "bimbo eruptions". Even when caught red-handed Bill lied until his entire house of lies fell down around his ears. He employed the old deny, deny, deny tactic but the conservatives would not let him off the hook. Bill claimed he did not have sexual relations with Monica Lewinsky. I'm here to say that if you use, expose, touch or allow to be touched any sexual areas of your anatomy in a sexual way that is sexual relations. Bill did acrobatic contortions to slither like the snake he is from under the questioning about his antics. Bill said it depends on what their definition of is is. Let me put it this way Bill: it is what it is! It's like saying I didn't eat the food I only chewed it. Conservatives throw their bad guys under the bus; liberals promote theirs. Liberals are appalled when conservatives do as liberals do. Continually deny and eventually the conservatives will tire of the lies and stonewalling and move on to the next new faux liberal crisis. Just as I stated earlier, liberals set the agenda and Republicans react to it. Let me remind you of the Rahm Emanuel quote from November 2008: "You never let a serious crisis go to waste. And what I mean by that it's an opportunity to do things you think you could not do before". At the time, Emmanuel was president-elect Obama's Chief of Staff. He is currently the mayor of Chicago. To liberals everything is a crisis. Each new crisis they conjure up is used to draw attention away from the mess they made out of the last crisis they made up.

Liberals cannot hold their own in a discussion that requires facts and truth to advance their argument. The only recourse they have is to resort to name-calling. When a conservative quotes a fact or undeniable truth and the liberal possesses neither, their righteous indignation kicks in and they "shoot the messenger". Liberals don't argue with facts, they change the subject. Liberals can't advance their argument using the truth because they are normally trying to hide the truth. The truth is: very few liberal programs or policies work when applied.

Most Americans believe bipartisanship means both major parties believe something in common. Not so for liberals. The liberal believes bipartisanship and compromise are achieved when conservatives give in to the way they think, which happens more often than not. When the liberals get just one RINO to vote for liberal legislation it is a bipartisan vote. No matter how many liberals vote for conservative legislation it is still reported as a party line vote.

Liberals are always beating the free-speech drum. The problem is that free speech as they see it is only free if it supports their opinions. Most American colleges are bastions of liberal free speech and endorse that idea wholeheartedly, which is why when a conservative guest is speaking on a college campus they are shouted down, have things thrown at them, and rarely stay long enough for the disruptive students and/or faculty to hear what they have to say. Free-speech on a liberal campus is a myth unless you speak "liberalese". If liberal ideas are the best available why do liberals feel the need to suppress differing ideas? Why wouldn't they let opposing ideas be heard in order to prove their liberal ideas are the best? Could it be because they know they aren't?

Liberals claim the moral high ground when it comes to tolerance of others. That could not be further from the truth. They claim that their party sits under the big tent that allows any and all to enter for the shade and comfort promised by liberalism. Admittedly, liberalism does attract a large and diverse following. Many reside in the dark of the big tent because their ideas are too insane to stand the light of day; many reside under the big tent because their petty grievances aren't worthy of a greater exposure; many reside under the tent because that is the only place they receive adequate sympathy for their victimhood; many reside under the big tent for no other reason than the fact that's where Santa Claus lives. No matter the status or purpose of their cause, there is no tolerance for opposing views. All the groups have specific agendas and they know the only way any of them will advance individually is by banding together and supporting the collective. A prime example of liberal intolerance is the disgusting treatment of black conservatives. Black conservatives must be discredited and destroyed simply because they don't fit the liberal mold.

Here are a couple more things we know about the differences between Conservatives and liberals: if a Conservative doesn't like the programming on the TV or radio he will change the channel; if the liberal doesn't like the programming on the TV or radio he will attempt to get that programming canceled; if the liberal can't get the programming canceled he will slander and vilify everyone involved in the programming; if a Conservative comes across a law or policy he feels has been unsuccessful and a waste of taxpayer money he will try to repeal the law; if a liberal comes across a law or policy he feels has been unsuccessful and a waste of taxpayer money he will waste more taxpayer money attempting to fix it; a Conservative enters a debate with the intentions of presenting truth and facts to sway his opponent; a liberal enters a debate knowing he has no truth or facts to debate with so will shout-down his opponent, call him names, or get him thrown out of the debate; a Conservative will try to reason with the liberal, a liberal wants to destroy the Conservative. When a conservative group like the Tea Party holds a rally, they clean up after themselves. When a liberal group like Occupy Wall Street holds a rally, they expect someone else to clean up after them. A lot of time is spent cleaning up liberal messes.

Establishment Republicans appear to have conceded to most liberal/socialist ideas. They don't seem to have the stomach or the spine required to advance Conservative policies. All they are interested in is staying in office and are content to be in the minority. Liberals on the other hand learned to manipulate and control Republicans simply by name-calling. Liberals have learned to use this successfully to shore up their base. The cry "racist" keeps the Black and Latino voters upset and hating Conservatives. The cry "homophobe" keeps the gays upset and hating Conservatives. The cry "sexist" keeps the women upset and hating Conservatives. Liberals don't care about the sensibilities of their base; they just need them to continue to cast their votes for liberals, which in turn keeps the Conservatives in line. Republicans are so conditioned to the liberal name-calling that each time it happens they slip under their desks and hide. Republicans should stand their ground and let the words roll off their backs, knowing the accusations are not true. They could defeat every hare-brained idea the liberals come up with. Make the liberals defend their policies in open debate rather than allowing them to stop debate by name-calling. If liberals had to disclose the truth about their agenda and outline their future for the American public, they would never win another election. Call their bluff!

Conservatives send their elected officials to Washington to represent them and to promote their agenda. The sad fact is that Republican voters are so naïve they continue to believe the politicians they elect actually end up doing that. Conservative politicians campaign to the right and they're mostly sincere in the promises they make but cave to the liberal agenda once they get to Washington DC. Very few Republican politicians manage to stand firm against the constant liberal onslaught of lies and slander leveled against them. If they continue to be intimidated by that, it will never change. Liberals expect their politicians to lie and cheat in order to be elected because "the ends justify the means". It is like the Islamic al-Taqiyya: it is okay to lie to nonbelievers in order to advance your ideology. Liberal politicians will campaign to the right and center in order to optimize their vote count but will legislate to the left when they get in office. Their liberal constituents know that and are okay with it.

Liberals never seem to consider the consequences of their liberal legislation even when Conservatives point out the possible negative outcomes. Everything is always unexpected. Liberals in Colorado passed legislation legalizing the use of marijuana but were taken by surprise by the unexpected increases in marijuana use by teenagers. Liberals were surprised by the unexpected loss of 40 hour per week jobs due to the implementation of Obamacare. Liberals were taken by surprise by the unexpected increase in fatherless households after 50 years of liberal giveaways enticing single mothers to have more children out of wedlock. Liberals were taken by surprise by the unexpected increase in male soldier on male soldier sexual assaults after dropping "don't ask, don't tell". Liberals were taken by surprise by gay divorces after legalizing gay marriage. Liberals (and some Republicans) were taken by surprise by the unexpected increase in illegals crossing into the United States after announcing amnesty will pass in 2014. These little surprises keep coming and coming. Liberals never consider the consequences of their feel-good policies. The most important thing to them is for everyone to believe that they care by virtue of having done something. It doesn't have to help, and seldom does, but they want credit for trying. Establishment Republicans have climbed onto that utopian-bound bus. They just want to be loved, regardless of who it hurts. That attitude is what will turn the Republican Party into a permanent political minority.

I want to talk about the glaring hypocrisy in how liberals perceive Conservative donors opposed to their own donors. Harry Reid's unhealthy obsession with the Koch brothers has morphed into a full-blown clinical psychosis. The definition of psychosis is: "the loss of contact with reality". It does not take a degree in psychology to see that Harry Reid has a serious and debilitating mental condition. The Koch brothers have to be demonized by liberals because they represent everything the liberals despise: they have achieved the ultimate American dream with hard work and want others to share in that dream with them. They employ tens of thousands of people and pay a couple of billion dollars in wages and benefits. They produce products that Americans want to buy. They do all this in spite of the interference by the federal government. They are Christian American patriots who believe in the exceptionalism of America. They are law abiding citizens but are labeled evil, rich bigots because they are Conservatives. The reason for all the liberal hatred: they donate millions of dollars in support of Conservative candidates and Conservative causes. To liberals that is blasphemy and the epitome of evil.

On the other hand, a liberal political donor has no faults. That donor can be as rich and evil as he likes with no backlash or criticism afforded him by the liberal recipients of his cash. A good case in point is a multibillionaire named George Soros. George is a Hungarian of Jewish descent. His real last name is Schwartz but he was a Nazi sympathizer in World War II. He is an atheist. He hates America. George is the rich crazy uncle the liberals love to accept cash from but hate to talk about as one of their own. What they don't like to talk about is the fact that George is a world-class crook and a convicted felon. George was convicted of insider trading in France in 2002. George is a hard-core socialist and is what is called a "citizen of the world". He is a manipulator of world currencies and has made a lot of money doing that. He loves to spend his cash promoting regime change and has been involved in four or five national revolutions and uprisings over the years. Soros donates billions of dollars to some of the worst organizations in the world and the more they hate America the better treatment they get from him. Soros never supports the cause if it doesn't benefit him financially. The more unrest and strife his cash generates the more he profits. Do your own research on Soros. There's plenty of information available about him. Go to the sites that praise him for his philanthropy and go to the sites that are less sympathetic to his causes. Weigh the differences and decide for yourselves. I've done my research and my conclusion is George Soros is not a good guy. That doesn't stop the liberals from accepting his money. A lot of time has been spent by Reid and other liberals complaining about the Koch brothers spending a lot of money in an effort to preserve America as we know it. Yet, Republicans spend no time at all talking about George Soros spending a lot of money in an effort to destroy America as we know it.

Another rich, but not evil, liberal cash cow is Tom Steyer. He made his money as an American hedge fund manager which would make him evil if he was a Conservative. Harry Reid stood at the podium on the Senate floor and said that Tom's reputation as a liberal donor and fundraiser was impeccable and above reproach. That is the same Harry Reid who stood at the same podium, on the same Senate floor, when he attacked the Koch brothers for doing the same things for Conservative causes. Some would call Harry a hypocrite but something tells me Harry doesn't have enough conscience to care. Did I mention that Tom is also a hard-core environmentalist? Can you imagine the liberals wetting their pants when they come across Tom at a Beltway fundraising cocktail party? I envision a puppy over-wagging his tail and peeing on the carpet when his new owner comes home from work. A couple other names that receive honorable mention for being liberal role models and donors and someone the liberals can look up to: Bill Gates and Warren Buffett. They have both made billions in the American capitalistic atmosphere that they both now donate cash to destroy. But since I'm not running for any liberal political office I really don't care about them or their money.

Let's mention a few more liberals and their social interference into areas that are none of their business. Michael Bloomberg was a liberal until 2001. He switched to Republican to run and win the mayoral position in New York City. As a Republican, he was, to say the very least, a very big disappointment. He was another example of a liberal campaigning to the right and governing to the left; very, very far left. His social engineering by banning transfats and sodas and salt were laughable but extremely irritating, not to mention an extremely large and expensive waste of New York City taxpayer money and time. Michael's successor, Commissar de Blasio, I mean Mayor de Blasio is going to make Bloomberg look like a lowly socialist dictator and the State of New York Governor Cuomo a second rate party wanna-be. Good luck New York; you voted for him; you got him elected; now you will regret that vote for a very long time. He is just getting warmed up. By the time he is done with you, the Empire State will look like a Third World country. He will coddle the criminals and abuse the law abiding citizens. Criminals will remain on the streets with you, not as criminals but as victims of the evil capitalistic society. As with Bloomberg, de Blasio will continue to drive out the wealthiest in your city with a suffocating tax structure.

Conservatives want to help Americans live a better life by allowing them as much freedom as possible to achieve it on their own. Taking care of yourself and your family is a patriotic thing to do and a serious self-esteem booster. If liberals allow you to survive their abortion gauntlet, they want to be in charge of every aspect of your life from "cradle-to-grave". They don't believe you are smart enough to accomplish life's tasks without their guidance and other people's money. The liberals don't spend their own money. The research I did pretty much across the board says Conservatives are 30% more charitable than liberals. That doesn't surprise me. Liberals buy taker's votes with maker's money. They then use those taker's votes to legislate new ways to get more money from the makers. I call that form of redistribution of wealth "Santa Claus Socialism".

# RINO

*"In matters of style, swim with the current; in matters of principle, stand like a rock."*
Thomas Jefferson

Republican In Name Only. I have always considered Republicans to be the most America-friendly political party. I was a little naïve in thinking they would always be true to the cause. I have now come to the conclusion that they will abandon the cause when it is beneficial for them to do so and that is what will make them a RINO. Also, if you spend more time and effort attempting to destroy the conservative members of your own base than you do defeating the liberals then you are definitely a RINO. Let me make an attempt to explain what I mean by "true to the cause". If you have a core set of values that you claim to live by you cannot abandon those values on a whim or they were not core values to begin with.

I know of a good Republican who is black who voted for Barack Obama simply because he wanted to vote for the first black president in US history. You cannot be a true conservative, regardless of race or gender, if you can so easily abandon your core principles. This man and Barack Obama appear to have no other similarities than race. He did not vote for Barack because he agreed with his policies or his ethics or his lack of experience, he voted for him because he was black. A true conservative is colorblind. A conservative does not vote based on skin color regardless of the color of his own skin. A conservative votes for the person that will best represent his views. You must remain true to your core principles under any circumstances or you are a RINO.

Does anyone besides me have a problem with South Carolina Representative Mick Mulvaney holding a town hall meeting and conducting the first hour of the meeting in Spanish? Why didn't he hold the first hour in English and the last hour in Spanish? On top of the glaring disrespect for the voters in his district, it turns out he was entirely supported by and road into office on the votes of the Tea Party. Oh how fast Washington power and money turns our elected officials into traitors to the cause. Does that sound like sour grapes? Does it sound like a racist rant? Call it what you want, but I'm tired of having to press 1 for English! Mick now qualifies for my RINO list.

I blame the establishment Republican RINOs for Obama's second term. Had they embraced the Tea Party patriots in 2012 Obama would not be in office today. I'm not a big Mitt Romney fan but he would've been a better president than Obama. In 2010, the Tea Party voted Republicans into a majority in the House. These people are the Conservative base of the Republican Party and yet the establishment Republicans rebuffed them. Republicans could be a nearly permanent majority if they would just except Tea Party support.

Now let's irritate some RINOs by name. I'm going to name names and give you a quick reason why they made my list. The list is not in descending order of the most offensive on top it is just who came to mind first. Actually, it may be based on that very thing. Whatever the reason for the order here's the list: John McCain, he never met a liberal he didn't want to write liberal legislation with, McCain-Feingold, amnesty; John Boehner, he never met a liberal he didn't want to cave into, debt limits, amnesty in 2014; Lindsey Graham, just wants to be John McCain's friend so he can have liberal friends too, trying to redeem himself by bull dogging the Benghazi scandal; Marco Rubio, for some misguided reason believes illegal alien amnesty is the answer to all the Republicans voting woes and it will have exactly the opposite effect; David Petraeus, recently said Hillary would be a wonderful president, I had previous doubts about his conservatism when he joined the Obama administration; Jan Brewer, abandoned her Christian values so the gays wouldn't call her names, I thought she was tougher; Chuck Hagel, went to the dark side by accepting an Obama cabinet post, but then he never was a true Republican; Colin Powell, never could quite get a grasp on Republican principles, voted for Obama; Mitt Romney, I never understood why anyone took him to be a serious Republican, his past is peppered with excursions into liberal leaning politics; John Roberts, he shouldn't be on this list since Supreme Court justices are not allowed to be partisan, but the contortions he put himself through to approve Obamacare in order for the liberals to like him is a typical RINO move so he makes the list; Mitch McConnell, this is a tough call because he continually makes conservative noises that confuse my judgment, but I honestly believe his hatred for the Tea Party will eventually push him over the edge. This list could be endless so I only covered what I would call "the cream of the crop".

RINOs and establishment Republicans take note: 17-year-old Saira Blair won a West Virginia House seat primary against her 67-year-old incumbent opponent Larry Lump. Her platform was pro-life, pro-gun, pro-family, and pro-capitalism. That conservative platform worked for her. If that conservative platform beat Mr. Lump, it makes a person wonder what platform he was running on as a Republican. Mr. Lump blamed his defeat on low voter turnout. I think he would've lost by an even larger margin had there been a high voter turnout! Conservatism wins elections when properly and sincerely applied by the candidate.

I mentioned it elsewhere in this book that establishment Republicans have got to stop their efforts to discredit their conservative base. Conservatives are not moving further right, establishment Republicans are moving to the left. They spend more time orchestrating the destruction of the Tea Party than they do the liberals. They are on the verge of again disenfranchising that very base in the 2014 and 2016 elections. Tea Party candidates or candidates supported by like-minded conservative groups have won a few primaries against establishment Republican incumbents and have lost a few primaries, by small margins, to other establishment Republican candidates. The RINOs have got to embrace conservative issues. They will continue to be losers at national political levels if they continue to embrace the same ideologies as the liberals they run against. Liberals have always adhered to the game plan of political destruction of their Republican opponents with cries of "racist", "bigot", etc. We now have establishment Republicans that are doing the same things to their own conservative candidates. Just recently in a primary runoff in Mississippi incumbent Republican Senator Thad Cochran used that very technique against his opponent Chris McDaniel. Cochran was supported by the establishment Republicans and McDaniel was supported by conservative groups such as the Tea Party. There was a large voter turnout because of the RINO/Tea Party implications that were conveyed by the national media. Cochran won by a mere two percentage points proving that the conservatives in Mississippi still have a voice and that voice needed to be heard. In an effort to assure his victory Mr. Cochran's campaign did robo-calling and sent out flyers to the black community which in essence called Mr. McDaniel a racist. His outreach worked; there are claims that an estimated 25-35,000 black Democrats crossed over to vote for Cochran in this Republican primary runoff. Cochran won by less than 8,000 votes and only by playing the "race card" against McDaniel. It's a sad day, and a very enlightening day, when an establishment Republican has to enlist the help of liberals to best his conservative opponent. Race-baiting and dirty tricks used against Republican opponents are no longer exclusively liberal campaign techniques.

Let me make this as clear as I possibly can in reference to the 2014 and 2016 elections. The actions of our Republican leaders in the summer of 2014 will have a lasting effect on the future of the Republican Party. In

2012 I stood in line at my voting precinct in the Florida sun for two and half hours to vote for a RINO. I won't do that again. What difference does it make which party candidate you vote for if you can't distinguish the difference between their respective ideologies? Do not think for a second that your conservative base will come out and vote for you if you pursue amnesty for illegals or back away from obtaining the truth about as many of the Obama administration scandals as possible and even prosecuting some guilty parties. Mr. Boehner, the disappointment in you over the lack of interest in prosecuting Lois Lerner, the person in charge during the IRS scandal, was palpable in my conservative circles. You will have to do some amazingly conservative things to regain our trust. Good luck!

In Thomas Jefferson's era they had a group of patriots that held a tea party in Boston. The tea party in Boston was in response to British tyranny based on excessive taxation and the unwillingness of the British king to acknowledge any form of American autonomy. The Tea Party of this era is responding to the failure of their party's leaders to push back against a liberal agenda including excessive taxation and their unwillingness to embrace their conservative base. The principle of rebellion is the same now as it was then. One last Thomas Jefferson quote: "A little rebellion now and then is a good thing, and as necessary in the political world as storms in the physical."

# VOTER FRAUD

*"The greatest threat to the constitutional right to vote is voter fraud."*

Lynn Westmoreland

Short of physical harm, committing voter fraud is one of the more repugnant things an American citizen can do to another American citizen. Simply put, voter fraud has the potential to affect every aspect of American life based on the policies of elected officials. If an official wins an election by fraudulent means everything that official does in office should be deemed fraudulent. Voter fraud has determined many elections in recent years and will continue to increase. Our liberal elected officials are okay with it and our Republican elected officials don't have the stomach to turn fraudulent voters into felons. It wouldn't take many cases of felony voters being "frog-marched" to jail in an orange jumpsuit to at least slow the fraudulent practice. The fraud will never be completely eliminated for a few different reasons. One reason is the rush to electronic voting. It is too easy to program voting machines to achieve a specific voting result. There are no "hanging chads" to count and recount. The numbers spit out by an electronic device are final. A second reason is having one political party entirely in control of specific voting precincts. Lost, misplaced, under-counted, and over-counted ballots as well as multiple voting are increasingly prevalent, especially in liberal voting precincts.

Liberal voter fraud is easily justified as a means to achieve victory for their candidates. It has been a common practice for so long that those few that are caught don't understand why they are in trouble. It is a standard for voting liberal that has been an unspoken practice throughout the generations. It's the liberal form of "don't ask, don't tell". Registering and voting for dead people is not uncommon. Voting multiple times by a single voter is not uncommon. In Cincinnati a lady named Melowese Richardson, who has been a poll worker for 25 years, admitted to voting for Obama twice in 2012. She insists she did nothing wrong. She felt that it was her democratic duty to help Mr. Obama stay in office. She was convicted of felony vote fraud and sentenced to five years in prison but ended up with probation. There is no doubt in my mind that she will do the exact same thing again because she was not punished for it when she was caught. I would guess that she still has her poll worker job to boot. Then again maybe not, as a convicted felon she is no longer allowed to vote. Make the prison term mandatory for everyone convicted of voter fraud; at least slow down the process and maybe even prevent it in many circumstances. It turns out her granddaughter, voting for the first time, also voted for Mr. Obama twice. It's like they always say: "teach them young". A North Carolina Democrat named Jim Turner posted on Twitter that he voted absentee ballot four times for Obama and intended to vote a fifth time on election day. He justified it by saying he hates Mitt Romney and feels he is saving American women from him. Jim also worked at his polling precinct registering voters. There is no indication that he was arrested or even questioned. It seems he was a big believer in the old voting adage: "vote early and vote often". These are only two of what I would suspect to be millions of similar cases. Liberals continue to win elections the old-fashioned way: they cheat.

In the 2012 presidential election 59 voting districts in Philadelphia voted 100% for Obama. How is it statistically possible that not one single voter picked Romney? In Cleveland 100 voting districts voted 99% for Obama. In a Milwaukee voting district 4,500 more votes were cast than the district had registered voters. A county in Ohio received 106,258 votes for Obama but there were only 98,213 eligible voters including Republicans. Those liberal precinct bosses had to get pretty creative to log an additional 8,000 votes for Obama. There is no end to these stories, all coincidentally, involving votes cast in liberal districts for liberal candidates. Voter fraud claims committed by Republicans are very rare. In Colorado, Florida and North Carolina electronic voting machines were automatically switching a Romney vote to a vote for Obama. That exposes the myth that electronic voting is more accurate and less susceptible to manipulation.

All this brings us to the solution to 99% of voter fraud: voter ID. Voter ID is the simplest and most effective method to prevent nearly all of the above abuses. There would still be a problem with electronic voting machines. Liberals are always squawking about "leveling the playing field" for all. Voter ID will do just that. No one has any advantage over anyone else if the voter is required to show proof that he is who he claims to be; one person equals one vote; fraudsters will be prevented from voting multiple times. The only way that works is for each state to establish and distribute legitimate voter registration information to the applicable voting precincts. Each precinct will then have a specific list of eligible voters for their district. Anyone attempting to vote other than at their specified district will be turned away. There will be instances where eligible voters are not on the voter rolls so they will need to file a provisional ballot that can be counted after their voter eligibility is confirmed. Counties and states all around the country have offered everyone and anyone a free photo ID for purposes of voting. If you can prove you are who you claim to be you can get the photo ID. You must have proof of social security number, a birth certificate, and any other pertinent information required by the ID-issuing authority. That is how simple the process can be to obtain a photo ID to vote.

Liberals claim having to show photo ID is equivalent to the Nazis asking to see your papers in occupied France during World War II or the Old Russian KGB requesting your papers to buy bread. There is no moral equivalence to that in voter ID. Kids have to show a birth certificate to join a Little League team. College students are required to show a photo student ID to attend college events. Law enforcement requires you to show a photo driver's license and proof of insurance papers when you get stopped in your vehicle. Are all of those requirements equivalent to Nazi or KGB requests? Try to get into Attorney General Eric Holder's office in Washington DC without showing a photo ID. Try to get into the NAACP's annual membership meeting without showing a photo ID. The NAACP required a photo ID to participate in a protest march in Raleigh, North Carolina. You guessed it; it was a march protesting North Carolina's requirement to show a photo ID to vote! The liberal hypocrisy never ends. They constantly trot out the old tried-and-true "racist" name-calling. They claim having to show voter ID will discriminate against minorities of color. That disingenuous claim is, in and of itself, racist.

There is no legitimate reason for liberals to fight with such ferocity to prevent voter ID implementation in the many states that have already legislated it or are in the process of doing so. The only purpose for opposing voter ID by liberals is to allow them to continue to win elections with voter fraud. Attorney General Eric Holder is using our Department of Justice to fight the implementation of voter ID laws in Texas and South Carolina. Liberal attack dogs are on the hunt and I sincerely hope that the conservative authorities in Texas and South Carolina can stand up to the intimidation and pressure brought to bear on them by their very own federal government. Maybe there's a light at the end of the tunnel. US District Court Judge Eric Melgren ruled that the federal Election Assistance Commission must allow Arizona and Kansas to require their citizens to show proof of citizenship when they register to vote. Let's hope that is the beginning of a trend. We need more judges like the Honorable Mr. Melgren. In actuality, many of the federal courts are overriding the voters in states that have passed voter ID laws in the past. That is more apt to be the future trend.

# CHURCH *vs.* STATE

*"Can the liberties of a nation be thought secure when we have removed their only firm basis, a conviction in the minds of the people that these liberties are of the gift of God; that they are not to be violated but with His wrath."*

Thomas Jefferson

*"I have wondered at times what the 10 Commandments would have looked like if Moses had run them through the U.S. Congress."*  Ronald Reagan

The so-called "Establishment Clause" in the First Amendment of the United States Constitution states: "Congress shall make no law respecting an establishment of religion..." This is the statement that the American Civil Liberties Union (ACLU) uses to sue government entities over prayer in schools and 10 Commandment monuments on courthouse lawns. I cannot understand how they read into that statement that an entity, who is not Congress, has made a law establishing a religion by merely praying or putting a monument on the lawn. You really have to contort yourself to come up with that interpretation. The part of the First Amendment of the United States Constitution that is called the "Free Exercise Clause" follows the establishment clause with this wording: "or prohibiting the free exercise thereof". Every time the ACLU or a school or a teacher or a town mayor prohibits a prayer they are violating the Constitution of the United States. They cannot prohibit the free exercise of religion but manage to do it at their discretion. How can those two statements be interpreted any differently than how they read? "Congress shall make no law respecting an establishment of religion or prohibiting the free exercise thereof." I'm no constitutional law expert, and judging by some of the sentence structure in this book, you know I did not do well in English class in reference to the grammatical breakdown of sentences. But in all honesty I have no problem interpreting what that sentence says: Congress cannot pass a law that establishes a state religion and they are not allowed to interfere with anyone in the free exercise of their religion. It doesn't get any simpler than that. There are no trick words to trip you up and no lines to read between. You have to be a complete illiterate to read that sentence and come up with the interpretation that the church and the state are in direct and perpetual conflict and are mutually exclusive of each other. This portion of Amendment One and the Civil Rights Amendment 14 are the bread-and-butter that the ACLU survives on. It seems rather hypocritical that the ACLU aims their wrath exclusively at Christianity. I've made my point and I'm done.

# CAPITALISM

*"Agriculture, manufactures, commerce and navigation, the four pillars of our prosperity are the most thriving when left most free to individual enterprise."*

Thomas Jefferson

I challenge anyone to point out a better economic or social system than capitalism. Scratch your head until you're bald; sleep on it until you can't sleep anymore; do any amount of Internet research you are comfortable with; read all the history of past failed societies; and you will not meet the challenge. The sad part about the hatred of capitalism is that it comes from two arenas: the liberal/socialist/communists that live in the system and those outside the system that are jealous of it. The dangerous part about the hatred of capitalism is the fact that the haters within the system are the most destructive. They are the ones that are typically called "the enemies within". Socialism, Fascism, Communism, and just run-of-the-mill dictatorships have only two classes of people: the rich and the poor. The rich will always be the ruling class and the poor will never have a chance to be anything except poor. Under capitalism there is a third group of people called the middle-class. The middle-class contains the poor people on their way to being rich which is exactly what capitalism promotes. No one remains poor if they have the ambition to better themselves. There is no minority poor that can possibly be held back unless they allow themselves to be. You can't advance if you sit and wait for opportunity to knock. Go in pursuit of the opportunities; work hard; you will be rewarded.

In a capitalistic system when a person reaches the top of an economic ladder they don't pull the ladder up behind them. They build a new and higher ladder for themselves and leave the lower ladder for others to climb up behind them.

Liberals coined the term "trickle-down economics" to describe Ronald Reagan's tax reduction policies. They believed it was simply a way for Reagan to give money back to his rich friends. Reagan firmly believed that tax cuts for the wealthy would give them more discretionary funds to spend which in turn would create jobs for others. So make fun of me too because I think that is exactly how capitalism works. Those with extra capital invest it in businesses that provide jobs for the middle-class or they purchase larger items from businesses that provide jobs for the middle-class. Regardless of the liberal naysayers, the Reagan tax cuts created millions of jobs and stimulated the sluggish Carter economy back to life. Either scenario allows the extra money to be earned by everyone. The increase in numbers of jobs and higher paying jobs puts more money in the tax coffers to be used by the government to help the less fortunate. Liberals should love what they coined "trickle-down economics" because it turned out to be a form of income redistribution, something they pray for to their gods. Reagan was ridiculed mercilessly but his tax cut policies started one of the longest and most successful economic upturns in the history of the US. Reagan proved tax cuts can be used as an economic stimulus, a fact that liberals simply choose to ignore.

Unlike liberals, normal people understand and embrace the tenets of capitalism: everyone has an equal opportunity to prosper; you are your only roadblock to achieving that prosperity. Unlike liberals, normal people realize that an unimpeded capitalistic system is inherently fairer to all parties involved than any socialist program they can put forward. What liberal/socialist elitists do understand is that their system allows them to prosper without working and requires all others to work without prospering. To those elitists, that is a level playing field.

One of the singular best attributes of America's capitalistic system is the intense love of competition. It does not matter what aspect of life is considered, competition dictates the achievement level reached. With no rewards for achievement mediocrity becomes the norm. That is true for business, sports, manufacturing, innovation, and even the quality of everyday life itself.

# ABORTION

*"Make no mistake, abortion-on-demand is not a right guaranteed by the Constitution. No serious scholar, including one disposed to agree with the Court's result, has argued that the framers of the Constitution intended to create such a right."*
Ronald Reagan

*"To compel a man to subsidize with his taxes the propagation of ideas which he disbelieves and abhors is sinful and tyrannical."* Thomas Jefferson (This is not about abortion but still appropriate.)

*"I've noticed that everyone who is for abortion is already born."*
Ronald Reagan

As of January 2014, 55 million American babies have been aborted since the Supreme Court ruling on Roe vs. Wade in 1973. I can't find any word in the English language that describes that fact more appropriately than "shameful". In the liberal world there is no shame in abortion. I'm going to make an exceedingly brash and sexist statement: If the liberals hadn't aborted 55 million potential liberal voters they wouldn't need amnesty to shore up their voter base. On top of that they could stop registering dead people and voting for them six times. I guess I am racist as well as brash and sexist. Oh well, liberals never look to the future to see the consequences of their actions. We are 41 years into the future and that averages well over 1 million aborted babies per year. We will never know if a future president was killed, a future fireman was killed, or the person that may have finally found a cure for the breast cancer that is associated with abortion.

If you have not yet figured out where I stand on abortion I will say this: I believe a life begins at conception. As soon as an egg is fertilized a human life is started. Abortion should be extremely rare. It should be allowed only in the case of rape, incest (which is rape), or the preservation of the mother's life. I realize that by allowing abortion under any circumstances is still abortion. There has to be rights preserved for the woman. The right to have an abortion as a form of birth control should not be one of the options. There are too many less disgusting options available to prevent pregnancy. I understand that stuff happens and girls get pregnant. But if getting pregnant wasn't so easy to fix with an abortion, maybe boys and girls would be more prudent in the way they approach sexual activity. Yes I am an old white man and should have no place or no say in the matter but I have the right to express my opinion about this godless activity. How the United States Supreme Court found the right of abortion in the Constitution is still a complete mystery to me. They had to contort themselves even more than John Roberts had to contort himself to find a constitutional basis for the establishment of Obamacare.

Planned Parenthood, the leading provider of abortions in America, has stated they are planning to spend $16 million on the 2014 midterm elections. You already know who is going to receive every nickel of the $16 million. You are correct: the liberals. The liberals provide taxpayer funding and political cover for Planned Parenthood and in turn Planned Parenthood returns the laundered taxpayer funds back to the liberals as campaign donations. Pretty slick gig, huh? We have an organization that has ended the lives of tens of millions of babies being funded by Conservative taxpayers who, in large part, hate abortion. The taxpayers have no say in their money being used to fund such a disgusting organization. Paying for abortions should not be forced on the American taxpayers. Abortion, as in the case of birth control pills, should be at the expense of the individual.

Do you remember the story about Scott Peterson in California who killed his eight months pregnant wife and was convicted of two counts of first-degree murder? If it was murder for Scott Peterson to kill an eight-month-old unborn child, why is it not murder when an abortion doctor does exactly the same thing? If you have never heard how the procedure of abortion works, and specifically partial-birth abortion, I will not describe it to you and I highly recommend that you avoid learning about the techniques. You would have nightmares for the rest of your life. The fact that liberals claim to do everything for "the children" and yet are the biggest champions and cheerleaders for abortion seems a little hypocritical to me. I have to assume when they claim to be protecting the children they mean only the children that have survived their abortion society.

Here are a few very disturbing statistics: in the state of Mississippi 72% of abortions are black babies; in New York in 2012 more black babies were aborted than were born; on a national level 70% of single mother births are to black girls; that is why abortion has been called "the black genocide"; it is way beyond time to stop and reverse these trends; Washington bureaucrats, if you want a worthwhile project do something about these statistics.

There seems to be a shortage of parents ready to adopt newborn American babies. If Hollywood celebrities alone would adopt American babies instead of going overseas to adopt their "designer babies" we would have enough parents to adopt many babies rather than abort them. And just a quick note while I'm on the topic of Hollywood babies, would you people please stop giving your innocent babies names that will get them beat up or laughed at every day of their lives through age 20?

# PAST PRESIDENTS

I'm going to rate our past presidents, in my opinion, from best to worst. I will also make a brief statement about each.

1. I consider Ronald Reagan to be the best president in my lifetime. He has remained the closest to being a true conservative of the nine on this list. His one stumble was his naïveté when it came to trusting the liberals with promises they made in return for the illegal immigrant amnesty that he allowed. He forced the downfall of the Soviet Union and engineered the longest economic upturn in American history.

2. George W. Bush is my second pick but he also stumbled off the conservative reservation with his leanings toward illegal immigrant amnesty. But his biggest blunder with the liberals was believing they had his back when all of them agreed with him that Saddam Hussein had weapons of mass destruction and that they should be taken away from him by force. They were at his back all right, just long enough to stab him and run like the rats they are.

3. I had trouble putting George H. W. Bush below his son George. This George's liberal blunder was committed in the last few months of his presidency by believing the liberals when they promised him they wouldn't push him to increase taxes. His statement "read my lips, no new taxes" cost him his reelection against Bill Clinton when he ultimately had to raise taxes to cover the mandated liberal programs. And I don't care what the political pundits say; he would have won reelection had Perot not taken nearly 20,000,000 votes off the table. Clinton won by less than 6 million votes. Fewer than a third of the 20 million that voted for Ross Perot were liberals. They leaned Republican and Libertarian and few members of either of those parties would have voted for Clinton. Bush would've won easily.

4. This pick is going to surprise most people but I feel I am justified in placing John F. Kennedy in this position. John Kennedy initiated tax reductions and made gallant and successful efforts to curtail or at least slow the progress of communism in his era, a job many liberals of the time were loath to do. He stopped the Russians from occupying Cuba merely by standing up to their bullying and calling their bluff, an extremely conservative thing to do. His actions may very well have contributed to his death. If John Kennedy were alive today he would at

least qualify for RINO status. I'm pretty sure that would make liberals eyes roll back.

5. Jerry Ford was a nondescript president. He was president during the worst economy since the Great Depression. His biggest claim to fame was the pardon of his old boss Richard Nixon. His biggest achievement was based on the fact that he didn't do much harm as president.

6. Speaking of Nixon, this is his place in the roster of nine. The credit for ending the Vietnam conflict must go to Nixon. Nixon turned out to be pretty shady based on the Watergate mess. The one bright spot is the fact that he had enough integrity left to resign the presidency rather than drag the American people through the agonizing ordeal of his impeachment.

7. We've cross into the lower side of my presidential picks with Bill Clinton. Bill was the recipient of much praise based on his perceived prowess for financial matters. Clinton got credit for welfare reform but the fact is that reform was forced on him by Republicans. Bill Clinton got credit for a thriving economy during his two terms but it was the lingering results of tax cuts made during the Reagan years. Bill Clinton's legacy was left on a blue dress worn by Monica Lewinsky.

8. Lyndon Johnson's claim to fame came in the form of social reforms by attempting to eliminate poverty and racial injustice. He failed at eliminating poverty but was able to establish the Civil Rights Act of 1964 with the help of Republican legislators. Lyndon Johnson escalated the Vietnam conflict to the point of no return. He got tens of thousands of American boys killed.

9. Jimmy Carter was without a doubt in my mind the worst president in my lifetime, until Barack Obama took office. Jimmy Carter almost single-handedly established the world terror network. He allowed the first radical Islamic mullahs to take over Iran and begin their endorsement, funding, and export of Islamic terrorism. The Islamic revolution began with the mullahs taking over the American Embassy in Tehran and taking more than 60 Americans hostage. They were held for 444 days and all Jimmy Carter did was approve a rescue mission that failed. The hostages were released immediately upon Ronald Reagan taking office in January 1981 because the mullahs knew their actions would not be tolerated by the new American president. Jimmy was a weak president concerning American standing around the world and domestic economic functions. His "fireside chats" with the American

people were pathetic, disrespectful, embarrassing, and condescending all rolled into one. There was a fossil fuel storage in the 70s because of his incompetence in the Middle East and the best he could do for the American people was to tell them to put on a sweater and sit closer to the fire. He has no regrets about going around the world and bad mouthing America to whoever will listen. I will give Jimmy and his wife Roslyn credit for their work with Habitat for Humanity International because not being in charge of the organization even Jimmy can't screw it up. Stick to pounding nails Jimmy.

Our current president, Barack Obama, is so special he commands an entire chapter of his own in this book.

# UNIONS

Unions, with their lofty pay scales and very generous benefit packages, along with state and federal corporate taxes and regulations, have shared equally in the loss of manufacturing and other blue-collar jobs in the United States. American manufacturers can no longer compete on the world market because of the cost of production and the sale price of their goods. Those are simple and indisputable facts. American manufacturing and technology has always been the best in the world. Many people believe Japan and China developed all the electronics technology. Not so, they produced it from American specifications that they obtained by any means necessary. They now own that market along with steel, textiles, plastic products, and many building supplies because they can sell it cheaper than American companies can. Of course all of the blame gets dumped on the greedy corporate owners by the unions and the government. Corporate greed is not responsible for closing factories on American soil. Textile, steel, and electrical component manufacturers cannot compete when the domestic costs of doing business are so exorbitant. That is not greed; that is a fact of business. American companies do move their manufacturing operations overseas to avoid high labor costs and excessive government taxes. That is not the standard. That is not greed; it is survival. Most manufacturers simply are forced out of business because of union and government greed. If you need visual proof of that statement take a drive through the Rust Belt of the US, from the abandoned steel mills in Pennsylvania to the shuttered automobile manufacturing plants in Detroit.

Even though, in my opinion, unions have pretty much outlived their usefulness they were originally established for honorable reasons. Fair Labor Practices and Child Labor Laws established by the federal government were also based on honorable reasons. Workers banded together in order to have a strong enough voice to negotiate with their employers for decent wages and safer working conditions, both were needed changes. Government originally sided with big business against the unions for political reasons: corporate bosses donated to their campaigns and workers didn't. On several occasions, government troops were sent in to break up worker strikes and union rallies with force. People even died. As the unions grew stronger, the government officials realized they could raise more money from unions than their corporate friends. When the union officials realized the amount of political influence they could lay claim to, they became increasingly more corrupt. To this day union corruption is prevalent and bribing government officials is merely a cost of doing business. If you doubt that, try to do a construction project in New York City, Boston, or Atlantic City. Get a large bag of cash ready because you will find a lot of palms that need greased. By the way, did you know that the current Teamster Union leader James P. Hoffa is the son of the infamous Teamster Union leader James R. Hoffa? Most corruption schemes are best kept in the family.

Unions would like to curb the technology that produces machinery that replaces humans. I sympathize with that. All I can say is that technology will march on and there will be fewer blue-collar, middle-class type jobs that will actually require a human to complete. Keep in mind, barring breakdowns due to poor maintenance, machines never call in sick; machines never have to sit home with a sick mother; machines don't talk back; machines never need an ego-stroking session; and machines never ever go on strike and picket out front to prevent customers from entering the business. That is a tough working standard for any human to match. Lighten up, I'm just kidding...sort of. I concede that there are many hard-working union members in the US. They are an integral part of our American working class and deserve our thanks for their hard work. But you must admit that the high profile and often criminally corrupt unions are the ones that get all the media attention. They're the bad apples in the union barrel that spoil it for the good union apples.

Public employees should never have been allowed to unionize or have collective bargaining for this very simple reason: all wage and benefit packages are awarded with one-sided negotiations. Negotiations involve taxpayer funded employees negotiating with taxpayer funded employees and everyone wins except the taxpayer who, by the way, has no voice in the negotiation process. If the party that provides the funding for wages and benefits is left out of the negotiating, there is no give-and-take, there's only take. It is not negotiating, it is an awards banquet. How many jobs have you had in your lifetime that allowed you to set your own wage and benefits package? Regulations written by civil servants to protect their civil servant jobs seem inappropriate to me. When you see government scandal after government scandal and no responsible party is ever terminated, it enhances the lack of trust for our taxpayer funded public employees. They may be removed from that employment position as a gesture of appeasement to critics but that employee will invariably reappear in some other capacity or in some other agency. Even in the rare instance when a government employee is terminated they normally will retain all their crony-awarded retirement and benefits. George S. Patton, a World War II Army General and hero, said: "A civil servant is sometimes like a broken cannon - it won't work and you can't fire it".

Even the granddaddy of liberal icons, Franklin D. Roosevelt, agrees with me that public employees should not be unionized. In 1937 FDR wrote this: "the process of collective bargaining…cannot be translated into the public service. A strike of public employees…is unthinkable and intolerable".

# PUBLIC EDUCATION

*"If the children are untaught, their ignorance and vices will in future life cost us much dearer and their consequences that would have done in their correction by good education."*                    Thomas Jefferson

*"Academics commit their pupils to the theater of the world, with just taste enough of learning to be alienated from industrial pursuits, and not enough to do service in the ranks of science."*                    Thomas Jefferson

Some of the best people I know are public school teachers. Some of the worst people I know are public school teachers. I have friends that are public school teachers that may not be friends after this chapter. There are teachers that are completely dedicated to the education and well-being of our children. There are teachers that go to school solely for the paycheck, benefits, and eventual taxpayer-funded retirement. I tire of hearing how poorly school teachers are paid even though their average salaries for 9 months are equivalent to, and in some cases better than, the average 12 month salaries of private industry employees. Where the comparison moves in the teacher's favor is in the benefits and retirement packages that the teachers unions have successfully negotiated, not to mention the fact the teacher only works 9-10 months of the year.

The two worst things to happen to children and taxpayers were the establishment of teachers unions and the policy of teacher tenure. Most school administrators are ex-teachers. With that in mind, negotiating salaries and benefits is like negotiating with yourself. You're going to agree with yourself and you're going to give yourself whatever you want. Most school board members are merely political figureheads that approve budgets for their school districts but have very little to do with establishing the priorities for the dollars spent in their district. That is done by the administrators that the board hires and typically overpays. If you want the teachers to get higher salaries have the exorbitantly paid administrators spread some of their wealth around. If you don't believe they are overpaid, research the salary of the top administrators in your school districts. Why is tenure only applicable in public service jobs? I asked the question now I'll answer it. Tenure allows public service employees, and I will use teachers since that is our current topic, to have protected employment status after only a few years of employment. In the case of teachers it is normally only five years. If a worthless teacher can hang in there for those five years it becomes nearly impossible to be rid of them later. There are few things the national teachers unions will allow to be used for termination of one of their members. A bad teacher is still a bad teacher no matter how long they've been a teacher. If everything is done in the public schools in behalf of the children, getting rid of a bad teacher should be a top priority.

Teachers unions constantly claim that everything they do is to benefit the children. I'm inclined to be skeptical about that. For instance, teachers claim that smaller classes allow children to learn better. I think the true reason is that it is more difficult and time-consuming for the teacher to grade more homework and tests. Teachers claim that outdoor activities at recess are bad for the children. I think the true reason is the teacher doesn't want to stand out in the heat or cold to monitor them. Teachers claim that summer vacation is beneficial to refreshing the children's brains thus allowing them to learn easier. But I think the true reason is the teacher wants that time off also. Teachers claim that homework is bad for the children. I think that the teachers hate grading homework. Teachers claim that the use of TVs and computers enhances the child's learning ability. I think the teachers like the fact that the Internet is the teacher but the human teacher gets the paycheck. The kids get too much TV and computers at home. I think that teachers hate math, science, literature, spelling, English studies, and phonics because it is difficult for them to teach topics that they themselves are not proficient in. Okay, I admit, most of that is strictly my opinion, but I guarantee you there are teachers out there that are saying to themselves: "He's talking about me". Actually that's probably a stretch. The number of teachers that read this book will be as scarce as hen's teeth.

Schools teach sex education to very young children; they traumatize children with stories about drowning polar bears; they preach about the disappearing rain forests; they scare the children with bogus stories of global warming to such an extent that all life on the coasts will soon drown; but they teach very little reading, writing, arithmetic, and no phonics. No wonder our education system is so poorly rated compared to much of the rest of the world. Go to the National Education Association website neatoday.org and read the article "Beyond PISA: How the US Ranks Internationally on Five Key Education Issues". The article goes into great detail to explain the causes of the US education system's pathetic international ranking. The article lays blame on everything and everyone except the people who run the system and the curriculum they push on the students. Instructional time with students, discipline issues, the public view of teachers, teacher salaries, and immigrant student population are all cited as culprits in the poor educational results of American schools. Let's pursue these items quickly. Lack of instructional time with students is a direct result of the liberal school systems pushing computers as a wonderful educational tool. Granted, discipline issues begin at the home, but what parent has the nerve to discipline a child at home knowing full well Child Services will be knocking on their door because the school system "ratted-them-out" for spanking the child. The public view of teachers and teacher salaries are in a way tied directly to each other. Teachers unions and the National Education Association (NEA) are continually harping to increase taxes to get them additional money which leaves a bad taste in the mouths of taxpayers. If I had anything to do with the education of American children I would be embarrassed to ask for more money to continue that pathetic performance. And lastly, the liberals that control the public school systems in America are the same liberals who are pro-illegal immigrant advocates. They are the ones that are directly responsible for the immigrant student population. For that reason, NEA has a lot of nerve to use that as a reason for their poor performance on behalf of our children.

At the behest of the teachers unions in New York City, Mayor DeBlasio decided to close four charter schools. I guess he was just looking out for the kid's best interest as socialists always do. The New York City teachers were embarrassed by the fact that the charter school graduates were far better educated than their own public school students. The charter schools are for poor children who have parents that care enough about their kids to get them in a better school. So it's even worse than just closing the schools and hurting kids, DeBlasio and the teachers unions are hurting poor kids. We should allow parents to take their children out of a failed public school and enroll them in a private school to allow them the opportunity for a proper education. The public school should be required to give up the taxpayer funding they received for a child and apply it directly to the private school tuition fees in behalf of that child. There are plenty of studies that indicate homeschooled children test better than public school children so leave the home-school parents alone to educate their own kids.

Stop allowing schools to drug our children instead of teaching them to behave. Schools force drugs like Ritalin on children with just minor behavioral problems and sometimes without parental consent. They don't want to spend time disciplining the child so they drug them into quiet submission. Discipline is an important part of every individual's life and should be taught at an early age. Granted, the discipline has to start at home. Even though the teachers are typically liberal and don't believe in any type of corporal punishment or are in fear of lawsuits initiated by parents that don't believe in any type of corporal punishment, someone amongst them must be an adult. They are not doing the child any favors by not requiring any form of punishment for bad behavior. That is becoming painfully and dangerously obvious in the actions of some of our young adults.

Staying with the discipline theme, children who are consistently disruptive in class should be removed from the classroom to allow the students who want to learn to have a quiet atmosphere for learning. If the student cannot be redeemed and continues to be disruptive then they should be moved to a permanent study hall atmosphere where they won't ruin their fellow student's chances for a good education. My first inclination was to suggest that they be permanently banned from the school system and given back to their parents to do with them as they please. But to some parents, school is nothing more than a free babysitter and the parents are not concerned about the child's welfare in or out of school. If you feel the need to keep them at the school give them comic books, coloring books and Legos to entertain them during the school day. They will not be allowed to associate with the other children at lunch, recess, school assemblies, extracurricular activities or any other activity pertinent to the education of the other students. If they discontinue their disruptive behavior they would be reinstated back into the classroom at the appropriate level determined by scholastic testing.

Eliminating letter and/or numerical grading, advanced level classes, virtually all forms of scholastic competition, and any form of personal achievement awards are all contributors to our failed education system in America. The schools are destroying every reason for the students to excel. At every level of achievement there needs to be some form of reward. A scholastic lapel pin, colored ribbon, or even just a pat on the head is necessary to show the student their hard work paid off. It is incentive for the achievers to continue to achieve and it is incentive for the non-achievers to achieve more. The liberal educational gurus who believe our children receive a better education without any competition or rewards are completely ignorant to the fact that they are stunting students development as future productive Americans. The reason the American capitalistic system has thrived for over 200 years is because achievement is rewarded and competition begets achievement. Our feel-good public school system is doing more harm to our students than good.

The NEA has long pushed an educational system called Common Core. It is a standardized curriculum and testing system that leaves no tolerance for educating America's children outside their specific and restrictive guidelines. That system completely eliminates the good teachers from being able to teach what they feel the children need to learn. It has become so mainstream over the last few years that even RINO Republicans like Jeb Bush and Mike Huckabee believe it is the educational system of the future. Michelle Malkin, a nationally syndicated columnist, has been a leader in the fight against Common Core. The light she has shown on the horrible aspects of the system has created a backlash that may very well be the death of that program. Ms. Malkin is a true Conservative and is not hindered in her opinions by political correctness. Even Mike Huckabee commented the name Common Core has become so "toxic" that the program should be renamed. He advocates keeping the system standards of education intact but try to conceal the system with a new name. In my opinion, advocating for Common Core disqualifies both Jeb Bush and Mike Huckabee from being Republican nominees for President of the United States. The education of our children is too important to leave in the hands of incompetent leaders. Our children are our future leaders. They are the ones who will determine the continuation or failure of the American Dream.

School systems need to get back to teaching the "3 R's": reading, (w)riting, and (a)rithmetic). Those of you out there who know what that means are probably more than 30 years old because it has been at least that long since the school systems taught on that basis. School systems these days are more apt to teach Ebonics than they are phonics. Schools spend more time and money teaching about the environment and the social injustices brought upon the earth and the earth's poorest inhabitants by their evil parents, grandparents, and mankind in general. They teach the kids about the inherent unfairness of our capitalistic economic system. They teach the kids that American corporations are evil even though those same corporations will be the children's employers at some point in their future. They teach students about the disappearing rain forests but they don't bother to get a globe out and show the students were those rain forests are located. Schools teach the students the destructive lies of so-called "man-made global warming" but nothing about how much of the dirty air and dirty water man has already cleaned up. Children in grades K-12 are taught to believe that mankind is evil and Mother Earth should be the child's only true god. Schools are intolerant to any student that doesn't adhere to the liberal agenda and ideology. Students are disciplined with suspensions, expulsions, and even arrest in handcuffs for such minor things as drawing a picture of a gun or hugging a teacher or another student. The liberal indoctrination/brainwashing must end. The problem is the kids leave high school after those 12 years of socialist brainwashing without the ability to think for themselves nor research facts on their own or the skills to obtain a decent paying job. If they have the means to go on to college their liberal indoctrination will be taken up and continued by tenured college professors who are mostly old hippies, socialists, communists, and even a few hippie/socialist/anarchist/domestic terrorists like Bill Ayers and Bernadine Dorhn in Chicago.

The liberal/socialist indoctrination continues even after the college years. Private and governmental liberals continually try to make the American population believe how evil and destructive the US is in relation to racial minorities, women, sexual minorities, and the rest of the world. Keep the population ignorant and guilt ridden and you keep the population dependent on the guidance and generosity of the cradle-to-grave liberal/socialist system. It has long been documented that one of the first and best ways to control the people is for the socialist or communist leaders to take complete control of the school systems requiring the children to be raised from the onset to toe the party line. It's beginning to feel a lot like that here in our own backyard.

One other quick thought: Rather than forgiving student loan debt that financially overburdened taxpayers will have to absorb, remove the governmental roadblocks from businesses that prevent them from providing jobs. The college graduates can then find jobs that will allow them to pay it back on their own.

# ANIMAL RIGHTS

*"A rattlesnake loose in the living room tends to end all discussion of animal-rights."*                                                          Lance Morrow

*"If God had not intended for us to eat animals, how come he made them out of meat?"*                                                               Sarah Palin

*"Every moving thing that liveth shall be meat for you..."*     Genesis 9:3

So according to the Bible God gives every animal to man for food.


I really did not like using "Animal Rights" for the title of this chapter but I didn't know what else to call it. I love animals for what I consider to be all the right reasons: cats and dogs are cute and for the most part lovable and loyal; horses and other equines are fun to ride and are valuable tools for ranching and hunting; cows, sheep, pigs, chickens, turkeys, rabbits, deer, elk, pheasants, and fish (the list goes on and on) are very tasty; beyond that list the remaining animals in nature are also there at man's pleasure. God put all the creatures on earth to be used as man deemed appropriate. If they were to be used to pull a plow or to be eaten, so be it. God intended man to use animals. All of the 10 Commandments refer to how man was to treat his fellow man; not a single commandment was written about how man was to treat the lesser creatures. Any laws in print pertaining to the treatment of animals are man's laws and not God's laws. With that in mind that does not afford animals human-style rights. That is why I was reluctant to use the title "Animal Rights". Brace up people, it gets worse from here.

I consider humans to be the top of the food chain in most situations. I consider humans to be part of the food chain when unarmed in bear country and in most water of the world. Many people have lost that perspective. It does not matter how many years cats and dogs and horses and parrots have been domesticated, they are wild animals at heart and can turn on you in an instant and for no apparent reason. Anyone that owns a dog of any breed and allows that dog around children is at best an idiot and at worst a child abuser. How many children have to be mauled and killed each year because the dog has rights? The pet owner says "My goodness, he's never done that before", pets him on the head and goes on about his life with little regard to scars and trauma that child bears for the rest of his/her life.

What does it say about a society that allows dogs or bears or killer whales to kill a human being without consequences for the animal? Maybe it would be a society that would themselves kill unborn humans without consequences. Would it be a society that allows animal-rights to overrule human rights? Would it be a society that would shut off water to farmers who grow food for humans in order to maintain a habitat for a worthless fish? Would it be a society that would value the presence of a burrowing owl over the need for the property owner to build a house for his family? Would it be a society that would protect tree owls against loggers that want to provide lumber to allow that homeowner to build a house for his family? Would it be a society that would spend millions of taxpayer dollars to build tunnels under roads to prevent migrating frogs from getting squished by cars? Would it be a society that would protect the habitat of a desert turtle in lieu of grazing cattle for human consumption? I could write an entire book about animal-rights trumping human rights.

Let's talk about endangered species. What a giant hoax the animal rights people have played on their fellow humans. Animal-rights people have somehow convinced the gullible that man is responsible each and every time a creature on earth goes extinct. Man's influence on animal extinctions, as with global warming, is so minimal it is not scientifically measurable. Man, as we know him, has only been on earth for several thousands of years. Animals had appeared and gone extinct by the millions before God ever put man on earth. Many millions of species of flora and fauna had survived or been lost without man's interference. If God intends for a particular species to go extinct, then let it go extinct. Stay out of God's business. Animal rights people claim that man has caused the extinction of animals but the fact is they cannot cite a single animal that has gone extinct specifically because of man.

Let's talk about the animal-rights advocates and what their stellar organizations are all about. HUMANEWATCH.ORG website states the Humane Society of the United States kills 3 to 4 million cats and dogs in their shelters each year. HSUS raises approximately $100 million per year but the bulk of that money goes to administration costs and not the care of pets. They still have a better track record than People for the Ethical Treatment of Animals. PETA kills 90% of cats and dogs at their shelters. Animal-rights organizations make sure that they get abused animals away from the human abusers. The abusers are fined and/or imprisoned. The animal lovers "rescue" the abused animals, take them back to their shelter facilities, and kill them. Sounds like reasonable justice for the abuser but not so much for the abused. These are the same people who protest the killing of mass murderers and condone the mass murder of babies. It seems they enjoy killing small things.

Not only are animal-rights activists hypocrites some are borderline lunatics. Swedish research studies determined dogs were happier if they earn treats rather than getting a treat as a handout. People like freebies, why don't dogs? I wonder if the questionnaire that made that determination was verbal or written. That's a silly question: it had to be verbal because dogs can't hold a #2 pencil to fill in the boxes. I hope that question-and-answer period will eventually appear on YouTube.

I have no idea who first came up with the idea of an alternate organization in direct contrast to PETA (People for the Ethical Treatment of Animals). The alternate PETA (People Eating Tasty Animals) is an organization I would be proud to take an oath to defend since I'm already a practicing advocate of the ideology. I found a website by that name but didn't go past the home page, but I will later. I enjoy comedian Ron White's take on the man-made climate crisis. His friend was talking about how cow flatulence was destroying the atmosphere and asked Ron White what he was doing to help the cause. Ron White's answer was: "I'm eating the cows". Keep up the good work, Ron. You too would qualify as a member of the alternate PETA.

# ENVIRONMENTALISM

*"If the federal government had been around when the Creator was putting His hand to this state, Indiana wouldn't be here. It'd still be waiting for an environmental impact statement."*                                        Ronald Reagan

I will start out by saying that having a watchdog with a specific cause is not necessarily a bad thing. Where that process goes wrong is when the watchdog teams up with the government to watch the citizens rather than the other way around. The environmentalists cause is rooted in good intentions. I have no bone to pick with an every day, garden-variety tree hugger. We probably have several beliefs in common. Where we part ways is when the tree hugger becomes physically violent. They burn down housing projects under construction; they burn down ski lodges; they vandalize heavy construction equipment; all these felonious acts are done with no regard to the toxins that are put into the very air and ground that they are claiming to protect. I'm not sure whether I should call that hypocrisy or just absolute ignorance. No matter which way you look at it, it turns out to be a combination of both.

I cannot understand what thought processes happen in their minds that will allow them to justify the destruction that they do. For some reason they seem to feel that what they do will prevent that activity from ever happening again. There must be loose wiring in their brains that causes cognitive thinking and common sense to go missing when they plan each raid. When they burn down a housing project under construction they don't stop that project, they delay it. They just wasted every resource that had been used to that point. There will now be additional fossil fuels burned, more trees cut down, and more iron ore dug up to replace what they just destroyed; that doesn't account for the amount of pollution put into the air and the space used in the landfill to dispose of the remnants of what they destroyed. I have friends that own heavy equipment they use to build roads in subdivisions. Earth First, one of the most radical and destructive environmental terrorist groups on the planet, trespassed on private property and vandalized a large earth mover. We know it was Earth First because, just like any two-bit vandal, they spray-painted their name on the side of the equipment. They cut holes in a couple of the 7 foot tall tires requiring new tires to be built and new pollution to be put into the air. They cut large steel-wrapped high-pressure oil lines. All those expensive oil lines had to be built new which caused new pollution to be put into the air. When they cut into the oil lines, a couple hundred gallons of hydraulic oil dumped directly on the ground requiring more energy to clean up a large area of dirt to prevent the oil from polluting the ground water. They caused the same pollution they were trying to stop. How can a sane person justify doing those things? If mummy and daddy would cut off their allowances, and they actually had to get a job to live, maybe they would have more respect for other people's property.

Let's talk about the liberal hypocrites in Hollywood. I smile at their ignorance when I see the enthusiasm these elitists exhibit when they promote environmentalism; the utter disdain they have for the so-called big business polluters around the US. It never occurs to them that their increasing numbers of "blockbuster action films" that feature the destruction of buildings, cars, airplanes, bridges, etc. with massive explosions are equally as detrimental to the environment as the job-producing big businesses that they rag on. These limousine liberals on the West Coast that own big mansions, private jets, three vacation homes around the world, take more vacations than the Obamas, all feel a superiority over the rest of us and our way of life. Living in California, "land of the fruits and nuts" has distorted their thought processes. Their make-believe profession becomes their make-believe reality. Stardom releases a smugness that is only equaled by the liberal hypocrites in Washington.

Our nation's capital, Washington DC, has a program called Leadership in Energy Design. The program is designed to rate new buildings on their energy efficiency. The buildings in this program use more energy than the buildings not in the program. The city has received several million dollars in fees from this failure but continues the bogus program for the money. Typical liberal think: "It doesn't matter if a policy works, it only matters that we tried, and it doesn't hurt if we get a little taxpayer money in the process".

Here's an example of two groups of liberal "do-gooders" eventually being at odds: birdwatchers and  environmentalists. Both groups love the fact that the Obama administration is stopping fossil fuel pipelines and the production at open pit coal mines and any other awful practice that may destroy a tree that a bird needs to live in. As with most liberal conservation policies there are always detrimental consequences. In this case, gasoline prices go up and electricity production without coal is more expensive, but the trees and the birds are okay. That is where the handholding ends. Massive solar farms are constructed on vast acres of land. Wind turbines spring up for as far as the eye can see. Environmentalists swoon, life is good. It's not so good for the birdwatchers and especially bad for their little feathered friends. We now hear reports about thousands of birds flying into wind turbines and being turned into avian sushi. What about the plight of the hapless bird that accidentally flies out over a solar array and is confused, blinded, and roasted before it hits the ground. I won't even discuss the sad future of the desert tortoise that now has to live in the shadow of a solar panel; life is cruel.

I chuckle when an electric car owner brags about doing his/her part to save the planet because he/she isn't using evil fossil fuels. Will the ignorance of these people never cease? Where does he/she think the electricity comes from when the electric car gets plugged in for recharge? Just a heads up: it comes from coal and natural gas power plants; both evil fossil fuels. But just to make you rest easier, you have a 13% chance the electricity for your car comes from a "green" source, but then again it may come from an evil, nasty nuclear plant.

There are several environmentalist groups in the United States that may actually have good intentions, but turn radical when the worship of Mother Earth clouds their thinking. It is not uncommon for many out there to wish a hand-to-mouth existence on the people of the world, but especially on American people. There are some out there that consider mankind a plague on earth that should be eradicated. I think they should start the process of eradication on themselves. That would be a very good place to start.

I'm not sure what genius came up with the 1.6 gallon per flush toilet. I'm equally not sure how many people this pertains to but I will take a wild stab and say probably 80% of the American population is affected by what I'm about to say. Reservoir tanks on toilets held 3 gallons of water before our genius came up with a plan to conserve water by making the size of the holding tank smaller. I personally have to flush twice to take care of business. I know, I know, that happens less than half the times I flush but hear me out. The 3 gallon tank shuts down after only 2 gallons because I don't have to hold the flush handle down. I have to hold the flush handle down both times I use the 1.6 gallon toilet which uses 3.2 gallons. I'm not seeing a big savings here. Sheryl Crow, the singer, once famously said that we should use only one square of tissue each time we do our business. I'm glad Cheryl has that option. If I used only one square of tissue I would have to take a bath using 30 gallons of hot water and a towel that was dried in the electric dryer just to clean up the mess. And what's even worse than that is the really thin recycled tissue that saves nothing because I end up having to use twice as much and possibly endure a breakthrough which would send me back for another bath and another towel from the laundry. Anticipating that breakthrough would be like dropping a hairdryer in your bathwater and hoping it pops the breaker before it electrocutes you. Not only have I used up additional Mother Earth energy and resources I used up all of my energy getting in and out of the bathtub. It's time to change the subject.

# CLIMATE CHANGE

*"Approximately 80% of our air pollution stems from hydrocarbons released by vegetation, so let's not go overboard in setting and enforcing tough emission standards from man-made sources."*
Ronald Reagan

The first thing I want to do here is point out that I absolutely believe in climate change. The seasons are the climate: spring, summer, fall, and winter. The weather changes by the minute, by the hour, by the day, by the month, by the season, by the year and in some specific lengths of time, such as seven-year climate cycles. The annual tilting of the earth, the sun's solar flares, and the moon's gravitational pull each have more influence on the earth's climate in one day than man has had in the many thousands of years of his existence on earth! Without any of the aforementioned influences, mankind and for that matter the earth itself, would instantly cease to exist. Who has the expertise, or the vanity, or the moral authority, to truthfully say with certainty that at this tiny moment in the history of the earth that we have the perfect climate? Any climate change the earth is experiencing right now has happened thousands and thousands of times over the years and in greater severity of heat and cold. In light of the billions of years of earth's existence it is not statistically possible that every climate scenario has not previously happened.

Millions, or even billions, of years ago the Earth's land masses were virtually covered with tropical vegetation. The year-round climate had to be considerably warmer than it is today. It had to be considerably warmer and wetter to sustain the flora and fauna all around the world. The reason we know those conditions existed so long ago is the fact that the flora and fauna are what Mother Nature turned into our current fossil fuels. The very fossil fuels that are presently found beneath virtually all areas on earth: deserts, under the oceans, tropical jungles, flatland prairies, and even glaciers.

Mother Nature has the ability do more climate change in one hour of volcanic eruption than man could ever conceive of doing. But, as God intended, Mother Nature also has the ability to heal any and all of her natural disasters with speed and grace. With equal speed and grace, Mother Nature also has the ability to heal any and all man-made disasters such as oil spills. Cases in point: the Exxon Valdez oil spill in Alaska, the BP oil spill in the Gulf of Mexico and Saddam Hussein's intentionally set oil rig fires. These were touted as the absolute end to all flora and fauna that existed in those areas. But lo and behold, after only a few years in each case, Mother Nature has taken care of the oil and returned the respective ecosystems to their original, pristine condition. After all, Mother Nature produced the oil in the first place. She knows how to control her offspring regardless of man's mistakes. As always, the arrogance of man leads him to believe that he has that type of influence on nature, good or bad. But, sadly, man will waste millions of hours and billions of dollars washing off a few otters and ducks to make himself feel righteous and during that process will waste more energy than he spilled in the first place. But that's okay, clean up as much as it takes to make you feel good about yourself then stay out of Mother Nature's way and leave her alone to take care of the rest!

The same "scientists", who in the 1970s, were predicting devastating global cooling to the point that we would have a new Ice Age are now predicting devastating global warming. Not just global cooling and warming, but man-made global cooling and warming. The same pollutants that were being put into the air in the 70s and causing global cooling by blocking the beneficial sun's rays from hitting the earth are now being put into the air and causing global warming by allowing the detrimental sun's rays to hit the earth. You can't have it both ways. Those of us who are not drinking the man-made global warming Kool-Aid are being dismissed as "flat-earthers". Why are skeptics not allowed to have an opinion? Our climate scientists are equally as intelligent as the climate change advocates scientists but with significantly less taxpayer funding.

With no discernible increase in global warming in the last 15 years, the "scientists" have come up with a reason for it: volcanic activity. The carbon ash and CO2 that volcanoes spew into the atmosphere is blocking the heat rays of the sun and preventing warming. But the carbon ash and CO2 that humans release into the atmosphere does not block the heat rays of the sun and does cause warming! Huh? I may be an ignorant ranch hand but I know you can't claim two entities doing the exact same thing will have exact opposite results.

Given the lack of warming in those 15 years and the last few winters here in the United States, I tend to believe the "scientists" were more accurate in the 1970s predictions. They were receiving taxpayer money paid out in the form of federal grants to say "man-made global cooling" in the 70s and are receiving taxpayer money paid out in the form of federal grants to say "man-made global warming" now. As has always been the case, follow the money. When the person or entity writing the checks expects your research to produce a specific result you do what they expect. If you are asked to prove man-made global warming exists in order to continue receiving taxpayer money paid out in the form of federal grants then that is the result you will come up with. The problem is these funds only flow in one direction. The government never spends taxpayer funds for, or requests, conflicting research that contradicts man-made global warming. That is precisely why the scientists that believe man-made warming is bunk are the ones to believe. They are not being paid to say it. Man-made global warming, regardless of what Al Gore says, is not irrefutable, settled science. Science is never irrefutable or settled. By its very definition science requires continual research. If the status quo prevails (no global warming) the government cannot convince the taxpayers that they produced a crisis and that they will have to fund the necessary corrections with additional taxes. If the people don't leave a large, so-called, "carbon footprint", the government loses the control necessary to tax the people in order to erase the footprint. Again, follow the money. Whew! It seemed like a long way around that bush!

There has never been a lack of attempts by man to alter the weather. I remember in high school in the late 1960s that the major ski areas in Colorado were "seeding" the clouds over Utah in an attempt to make it snow on their slopes. It snowed all right, in Kansas! It was exactly the type of snow the ski resorts wanted: powdery and deep. It was the perfect snow for skiing, but not for the survival of cattle. The snow was so deep and the storms so severe that the ranchers in Kansas could not get to their cattle to feed or water them and the cattle either froze to death or died of starvation and lack of water! In this litigious society I would guess that those lawsuits are still ongoing. I would also guess that cloud seeding is also ongoing.

There are more ongoing attempts at climate change. Some "climate scientists" recommend sending a giant sail into the atmosphere to lessen the effect the sun's rays have on the warming of the earth. So they finally realized that the sun may be what is warming the earth? It was about time they figured that out. If we block the life-giving sun's rays will that not eventually cool the earth to the point that life is not sustainable in an ice age? Can we assume the federal government will spend taxpayer funds to retain a sun shade company to make this shade roll up every once in a while and allow the sun's rays through in order to sustain life? Won't the massive amount of space debris tear it up? Won't the millions of small meteorites burn holes in it? Where will the trillions of dollars come from to build it?

If we had had 78,000 wind turbines off the coast of New Orleans they would have prevented 79% of the losses incurred during Hurricane Katrina, so say the same scientists that predict the demise of earth because of man's polluting ways.

Another "climate scientist" proposed a massive cloud of orbiting white golf balls to reflect the sun's rays. WOW! And they are not done. There is never a lack of geo-engineering solutions to man-made global warming and of course it will be man that has to correct all this. Rongjia Tao of Temple University has another great idea that will affect climate by lessening the effects of tornadoes across the Midwest. The idea is to build three walls east and west in various locations in tornado alley to disrupt the formation of tornadoes. These walls will be 1000 feet high and one hundred and fifty feet wide and will cost a mere $60 billion per hundred miles. I'm not sure how many hundreds of miles each wall will have to be and if Mr. Tao is honest, he probably doesn't know either! If you put the taxpayer-funded federal government and national unions in charge of construction expect that cost to be a 100 times that per 100 miles. Taxpayer-funded government projects, regardless of type or scope, never come in on budget or on time. Now let's cover a few more of the unintended environmental consequences: I'm no "climate scientist" but I know enough to say with some certainty that rain and snow patterns outside tornado season will also be seriously affected by three, 1000 foot, 100+ mile long walls; the migratory patterns of birds will be affected by the walls; the migratory patterns of landlubbers such as frogs, lizards, rabbits, man, et al will also be affected but easily dealt with via tunnels if you can find an effective way to herd frogs, lizards, and rabbits to a specific tunnel location; the appropriation of the land necessary to build these walls will be a simple process of government confiscation of private property affectionately known as eminent domain; the problem being that the government confiscated property will be some of the most productive farm ground in the world; loss of the revenue from the farm ground will be felt not only by the farmer but by the local taxing entities when the properties will be removed from the tax rolls. The only upside I perceive from such an ill-conceived plan would be that if it worked, and that is a big "If", there may be many lives saved and the prevention of severe property destruction. But on top of all this, who in their right mind would want the job of changing the bulbs in the aircraft warning lights or painting it every seven years?

"Climate scientist" James Lovelock has announced that it is too late to save the entire planet and our only hope of survival is for everyone to retreat to climate-controlled cities. He claims that saving the planet is beyond our abilities. I say destroying the planet is beyond our abilities. Take your meds James and the last few years of your life will be more pleasant. Mr. Lovelock made these comments around 2006. Recently Mr. Lovelock has distanced himself from his regular kook crowd and may have redeemed himself somewhat with normal people by rejecting renewable energy sources such as solar and wind as "hopelessly inefficient and unpleasant". He was especially harsh on wind farms as "ugly and useless". He also retracts his previous idea of abandonment of the wilds for city living by saying he was an "alarmist" (no argument from me about that, James). Good for him for seeing the light but bad for his career. I bet his head is still spinning from the speed at which he was unfriended on Facebook. Will the ignorance of the do-gooders ever end?

The antics of the global warming crowd never fail to amuse me. I always draw some sadistic amusement each time the global warming crowd decides to have a "save the earth from man-made global warming" summit and it snows on them! I laughed out loud each time I watched in December 2013 (December is Antarctic summer) when the ship the man-made global warming advocates were on in the Antarctic got stuck in the ice. They were there attempting to prove the disappearance of the Antarctic ice cap was a result of man-made global warming. I fell off the couch, with tears in my eyes, and nearly wet my pants laughing as I watched in complete amusement when the icebreaker sent to rescue them also got stuck in the ice! You just can't make this stuff up.

On the other hand, the bulk of the data coming from the global warming crowd are made up, erroneous, false, inaccurate, extremely irritating, occasionally dangerous, and always detrimental to the world economy. In the short time of man's existence, there have been very few more disingenuous scenarios presented to man than those representing man-made global warming. One of the most glaring examples of this came to light in 2009 when two members of the United Nations IPCC (Intergovernmental Panel on Climate Change)"climate scientists" at the Climate Research Unit and the University of East Anglia had their emails hacked. The emails revealed that the scientists manipulated the climate data they used to support their global warming theories and made all attempts to suppress their critic's rebuttals of the results of their false data. If you would like to research this particular tidbit of bogus global warming data do a web search for "Climategate". These gentlemen of the IPCC are the high level, overpaid climate gurus that are hand-picked by the United Nations dictators and thugs to push this false, man-made global warming crisis in order to create a global taxing base to benefit themselves, their families, and their corrupt governments.

The method to be used will be the creation of carbon credits that can be bought and sold or traded on the world market to offset or totally eliminate the pollution (carbon footprint) that is produced by the offender's country or business or both. The revenue stream that will be made available to the United Nations will be based on a tax levied on all the global nations and based on the so-called "carbon footprint" of each nation. Of course the size of the "carbon footprint" and the tax will be determined by the United Nations. You know as well as I that the United States of America will take the largest tax hit and will pay the bulk of the tax revenue. The world dictators who actually produce the bulk of the pollution would like nothing more than this carbon tax collected from the United States that would represent an unlimited slush-fund to be used by the dictators to sustain their dictatorships.

Global warming advocates use computers that have been fed "worst-case scenario" data by those same advocates in order to obtain their alarmist results. The results are intended to shame the "sheeple" and compound the shame by scaring their small children into hating their parents for killing all the cuddly polar bears. These same "climate scientists" cannot predict with much accuracy what the weather is going to be the following morning but we should take their word for what will be happening on earth 100 years from now. I just don't buy it. All attempts to use facts and historical climate data have failed to convince the global warming crowd that man has very little to do with climate change or that we could have a lasting effect on the Earth's future climate. If you want honest and accurate climate information research Roy Spencer, a climatologist at the University of Alabama at Huntsville.

I have spent considerable time picking on climate change enthusiasts in general. Let's now take some time to expose the hypocrisy of their big kahuna and almighty guru, Al Gore. There's so much to expose that it is difficult to determine where to start. Let's start by talking about Al Gore's extensive travels. He continuously travels around the world (in private jets) and is paid to attend man-made global warming conferences. At these conferences he chastises the world population for their pathetic conservation lifestyles and wasteful use of fossil fuels, exactly the same fossil fuels that are burned in the private jets that he, himself, travels in. You could cut the hypocrisy with a knife. But Al Gore is the guru and the guru must travel in order to service his following.

Let's move on to his palatial properties. There are two that I am aware of and each uses the amount of energy necessary to sustain some small towns. His primary home is a 20 room mansion in the exclusive Belle Meade area of Nashville. It has 20 rooms and a guesthouse. I guess there are not enough rooms for the guests in the main house. He did some environmentally friendly renovations a few years back which included switching all his incandescent light bulbs to compact fluorescent bulbs and installing some solar panels on the roof. Those renovations resulted in an 11% reduction in energy consumption. Kudos, Al. His other mansion is a $9 million, 6,500 square foot, six bedroom, nine bathroom, ocean view mansion in Montecito, California. Both of these properties are absolutely necessary to maintain the bachelor lifestyle that he has grown accustomed to.

His carbon footprint is extensive and requires massive numbers of carbon credits to offset his carbon usage. Al has a solution to his carbon usage problem. Just by coincidence Al Gore is a co-owner of a global company that sells carbon credits! The company is called Generation Investment Management and has netted the two owners hundreds of millions of dollars in carbon commodities sales. Al Gore has amassed a very large fortune selling these worthless carbon credit chits. Al is not the smartest man when it comes to climate change or global warming which is his "inconvenient truth". But he is without a doubt the best snake oil salesman on the planet.

One more quick tidbit just in case you weren't aware of it. Al Gore owned a large stake in a cable tv network called Current TV. When it came time for Al Gore to sell the cable channel Glenn Beck, of The Blaze radio and tv fame, made an offer to purchase it. In order to protect the seven faithful followers of the channel Al made the decision not to sell the network to a nonbeliever. Even though Al has spent his entire adult life hating and disrespecting oil producers he decided it was best to sell to Al Jazeera Satellite Network who, by the way, is owned by Arab oil producers in Qatar. Al netted a cool $70 million on the sale. No irony or hypocrisy on your part, right Al? Al lives well and will continue to live well at the expense of the little guy so long as there are people gullible enough to continue to buy his lies, his carbon credits, his movies, and his books; in short: his snake oil.

Okay, okay, I'm not done dissing Al. When not jetting around the world in fuel guzzling private jets, Al rides around on terra firma in gas guzzling limousines and SUVs. One of his drivers was noticed waiting in a vehicle with the engine running. The reason: So that Al would not have to get into a hot vehicle after his lengthy meeting. I keep going because the hypocrisy keeps going. Did you know Al Gore owns a fuel guzzling yacht? It was built for him by the famous luxury yacht builder Bill Austin of Sparta, Tennessee. The 100 foot yacht/houseboat is docked at Hurricane Marina in Smithville, Tennessee. The name of the yacht is "Bio-Solar One" because it runs on bio-diesel and has solar panels on the roof. I have to assume Al uses the yacht as a stationary party house because there is no bio-diesel available anywhere on the lake where the yacht is docked. Only a climate brainiac like Al Gore could create a situation like that and expect no one to notice.

The Obama global warming groupies are going after dairy cow flatulence and belching. I read a nice, one-sided article about how detrimental dairy cow emissions of methane gas can be regardless of which end of the cow is emitting it. They are considering regulations requiring the dairy farmers to develop ways to capture the gas thereby preventing it entering the atmosphere and causing further, evil global warming. It seems the farmers are on their own to develop this technology. The federal government, under Obama, has wasted billions upon billions of taxpayer dollars for questionable research and development of sustainable energy sources at the companies of his political donors. Why can't they spend taxpayer dollars helping the farmers with their emissions dilemma? I've been around farm animals for about 50 years of my life. Maybe I can help where the federal government won't. I envision a large platform mounted on the back of the cow and held in place by large underbelly straps. On the platform will be a methane gas compressor and an appropriately small, pressurized holding tank. There will be a collection hose to the muzzle of the cow that attaches to a nose mask that collects the belched methane gas. There is another hose going to the opposite end of the cow attached to a diaper looking apparatus strapped to the cow's tail region. I'm having a little problem figuring out how to get a tight seal at that end of the cow short of inserting the tube directly into place, but that's merely an engineering detail. When the cows are brought in twice a day for milking the holding tank's contents are transferred to a larger storage tank. This system will work for cows that are confined and attended to daily but will not work for free range cattle. My solution to that would be to move the apparatus from the back platform to a pull-behind cart thus insuring the cow would maintain its mobility. The cow would be harnessed to the cart in the same fashion as a horse or mule to a cart. But then addressing horse and mule flatulence is for another day. With the pull-behind cart we could install a larger holding tank negating the need for daily purging. In feedlots there would be a large number of hoses hanging from an overhead collection system. Each pair of hoses would be attached to a single cow thus allowing them to roam freely in the lot. The hoses would tangle but that again is just another engineering detail. So is everyone straight? I have a solution to the problem. At least I have offered a solution which is more than what the global warming kooks have done, until recently.

Note: I wrote the above paragraph with my engineering solutions to the problem a few months before I read the article about the federal government's renewed concerns about cattle flatulence. Lo and behold, someone came up with the exact plan, or at least the idea of putting tanks on the cows. Now everyone knows that you can't just capture the methane in a tank, you'll have to compress it into the tank, thus requiring a compressor which is one of my engineered components of collection and storage. Anyway, I wrote my notes tongue-in-cheek and with all comedic intent. Now that the Obama people have determined that my idea is a viable solution to the cow flatulence problem, and the cat is now out of the bag, I kick myself for not having patented this apparatus. It may be worth billions.

Can man pollute the low atmosphere directly above a specific area of the earth such as a city? The answer to that is: "yes". A limited area of temperature inversion, with the lack of wind, and an abundance of auto emissions and burning fossil fuels can produce localized smog. That localized smog can extend for many miles but will eventually be dispersed by Mother Nature. Those emissions and smoke are carbon-based as are nearly all life-forms on earth including humans. Carbon is a naturally-occurring component necessary to sustain all life on earth. Man did not make this stuff up, nature did.

Who can say that a 2° rise in average temperature would not be beneficial to the earth? Man would have longer growing seasons allowing him to feed the increasing billions of mouths. It would take less fossil fuel to heat homes but it would take more to cool homes so that would be a wash. Because of the rising water levels resulting from the melting ice caps there would be fewer beaches in their present locations, but there would be new beaches further inland. Since it would be hotter, there would be a smaller demand for beach property but there would be a larger demand on the cool mountain property. For the people that own both, it would also be a wash. Another advantage to the melting ice caps would be the global warming enthusiasts would not get caught in Antarctic's summer ice again. And last but not least, who but a few liberals would mourn the loss of Miami Beach, San Diego, and New York City's waterfront? All I ask is "Please keep Lady Liberty's feet dry".

2013 was the third year in a row that the Midwest experienced fewer tornadoes and the Al Goreites cry "but the ones we got were more destructive". If we stop having tornadoes altogether what would be their cry "we need more tornadoes to slow the population growth"? The reason I make that comment is because the global warming crowd also believes that man is a blight on earth and should be eliminated. Their god is Mother Earth and she should be protected from man at all costs.

According to the National Climate Data Center as of March 29, 2014, 2,071 new record lows were set in the United States and only 242 record highs. Looks to me like the new Ice Age is winning!

There is no scientific proof that man-made global warming is happening. All of the so-called evidence of such is produced by computer models. The computers base their climate models on flawed information fed to them by taxpayer-funded "climate scientists". Everyone remembers the old computer adage: "garbage in-garbage out". The world's population is no longer drinking the Kool-Aid. The believers frustration level has reached its peak. Pay special attention to the last few speeches that Al Gore has given. Also, when John Kerry says: "neither he nor the president will waste one more minute talking to flat-earthers", that means they no longer have any BS in support of the cause.

# ENERGY

*"You must remember to compare benefits versus costs. For the foreseeable future, the only affordable alternatives are coal, natural gas, oil or nuclear. Renewable sources - solar, wind, etc. - so favored by the left remain prohibitively expensive. A nation becomes weaker, not stronger, by artificially overspending on costly, inefficient alternatives to fossil fuels."*

Larry Elder

The United States has more oil and natural gas than is available in all of the Middle Eastern countries combined. The United States has more and cleaner coal than most coal producing countries of the world. If the environmentalists, the EPA, and the current US Administration would get out of the way and allow those resources to be extracted and used here in the United States, we could be 100% independent of foreign energy in a very short timeframe.

There is no excuse for continued use of foreign energy. Energy dollars that would stay in America would be the answer to America's financial woes. Our in-house energy production would have a wide and positive effect on the American economy including, but not limited to, more and higher paying jobs along with a reduction in the cost of consumer goods. If you can't draw that conclusion from looking at the Dakotas and Texas than there is something seriously wrong with your cognitive powers. There would be no limit to the economic advancements that would be made possible by reasonably priced energy. Energy is life. Without energy nothing moves; nothing is manufactured; no commercial buildings or residential dwellings would be heated, cooled or lit or even built; no food would be produced; no life-giving water would be pumped; life as we know it would cease to exist. Actually, all of the above things would still happen, but it would take a lot of sweat, blisters and groaning to make them happen. We would be reduced to subsistence living; that means that you would be required to feed and shelter yourselves on a 24/7 basis. No TV, no DVD, and no trip to the supermarket to buy your food. Americans have become so secure in their way of life most have no clue that the above scenario is not only likely in our future but probable. When the economy gets so bad that you have to choose between paying your electricity bill or feeding your children the choice will be simple. You will have Mr. Obama to thank for having to turn the lights off.

The Keystone pipeline, the pipeline that Obama has successfully slowed to a crawl, would produce a fairly large but temporary revenue boost to those involved in its construction. I am not quite so enthusiastic about the ultimate destination of the Canadian oil not being the United States. The oil will be refined at Texas refineries but the bulk of the resulting products will be shipped overseas. There of course will be many steady jobs on pipeline maintenance and in US refineries. We will reap some benefit from the oil piped across the US but the bulk of the benefit will be to the Canadian oil producers who will now have access to American refineries and American seaports. I would hope that there would be an agreement with the Canadians that would require some percentage of the refined products to be made available to American consumers at a reasonable price. Under any circumstances I would still prefer purchasing oil from our neighbors, Canada and Mexico, than any other source. Besides, closer oil has to be cheaper oil, right?

I want to discuss further Mr. Obama's blocking of oil, gas, and coal production. His ultimate goal of reducing the United States to a Third World economy from the world's only superpower will be achieved by his never-ending quest to destroy our energy production infrastructure. There is no easier way to destroy energy production than by denying permits to extract the resources. The ultimate insult is denying permits to extract resources from taxpayer owned land. We will not be able to compete on a world market if our energy costs exceed our selling price. There is no better way to stifle an economy than with expensive or unavailable energy.

Another big advantage to ending American dollars going overseas would be to slow down the amount of terrorist activities around the world that are funded by rogue nation oil. Nations such as Russia, Venezuela, Iran, and a never ending list of terror supporting, Middle Eastern countries would see a major drop in energy revenues. That would make the dictators think twice about wasting their money on something other than themselves.

As a sideline to this energy topic I want to drift into energy and commodity consumption. In order to increase or even maintain our standard of living the United States must consume an extremely large amount of energy and other resources. I will make no attempt to deny that fact. What I will deny is the finger-pointing done by those inside and outside the US that claim we rape the rest of the world's economies and resources in our "selfish and gluttonous" pursuit of our elevated standard of living. We Americans have worked harder than any other population in the world to achieve what we have. We have worked longer hours; we have worked smarter, we have been more innovative and sacrificed more in that pursuit. I will not feel sorry for others who haven't and I will not apologize for the standard of living that Americans have achieved. We have done it cleaner and more efficiently than any other country. We set standards for clean air, clean water, safer working conditions, product quality, and we are continually improving all those standards. No other country on earth can match those standards.

When we buy commodities on the world market we pay whatever the seller of the commodity asks and we take possession. A willing seller and a willing buyer are both necessary to complete the sales transaction. If you don't want to sell your products to us, you don't have to sell them to us. We can go elsewhere on the world market and make our purchases. Sellers have the option to sell to anyone they please. They also have the option to refuse to sell to anyone they please. There are those who will cry "foul" no matter how many American dollars they stuff in their pockets. Envy is a sad state to find yourself in.

Continuing on with consumption, Obama has taken it upon himself to raise the Corporate Average Fuel Economy (CAFE) standards on trucks and SUVs that will be available in the United States in the near future. The standards will begin going into effect in a few short years and are completely unrealistic. The ultimate goal of these new standards is to force the manufacturers to discontinue the production of the trucks and SUVs because it will not be possible for the manufacture to meet the standards. They cannot presently produce cars that consistently meet those standards. There will be many Americans, myself included, that will not willingly give up the safety of an SUV for a small, light-weight deathtrap. I guess we could be buried in them, thus saving the cost of a coffin. One of the easiest ways for a car manufacturer to lower fuel consumption in vehicles in order to achieve federal standards is to lower the weight of the vehicle; use less metal and more plastic in the production of the vehicles. Remember when toy cars were made out of metal? They have gradually become plastic. There was no purpose to doing that other than being able to make the toy cars cheaper because safety wasn't an issue. Turning our on-the-road vehicles into small plastic deathtraps is definitely a safety issue.

Let's do some math. Obama claims his new CAFE standards will cut your gasoline bill in half and save you $8, 000 a year by 2025. That means you will be paying $8,000 for gasoline in 2025. If the average miles driven by you, per year, remains at about 12,000 and your new vehicle gets 40 miles per gallon you will use 300 (12,000 miles ÷40 mpg) gallons of gas for the year 2025. If you divide the $8,000 Obama says you will spend on gas by the 300 gallons you use, the cost of gasoline will be $26.67 per gallon ($8,000 divided by 300 gallons used). Ouch! The sad truth is if the economy continues its downward spiral (there is no reason to believe Obama and his successors will make any effort to stop it) and double-digit inflation eventually kicks in, gasoline will easily cost $26.67 per gallon by the year 2025. Either Obama picked the $8,000 out of the air or he seriously screwed up by disclosing that he and his comrades hope the $26.67 per gallon gasoline will deter consumption. Even when he's not lying outright he manages to lie by omission.

The last point I would like to make is how detrimental Mr. Obama's energy policies are to the American economy. Everyone squeals about the high cost of gasoline and heating fuel but no one complains about the obvious destruction of our fossil fuel production in the United States. We will never be independent of foreign oil by erecting wind turbines and solar arrays. We do not have the technology to produce the amount of power necessary to cover the American needs. There doesn't seem to be the technological advances in the foreseeable future that will allow the energy to be produced by those means and be financially feasible. The amount of taxpayer money being wasted in the fairytale pursuit of "green energy" alternatives is astonishing.

# MIDDLE EAST

*"The evidence of a Jewish civilization going back more than two millennium is overwhelmingly borne out in the archaeology of the region. The heritage of the Jews in Palestine is documented."*
                                                                    Jack Schwartz

God called the land that is now Israel "The Promised Land" and gave it to the Jews. He made them wander the desert for 40 years before he deemed them worthy of the land. I believe he picked that area with the idea in mind that it was so desolate no one else would want it and thereby leave the Jews to live there in peace. It didn't work out that way. The Jews lived on the land for almost 2 thousand years prior to occupation by the British Empire. In November 1947 the United Nations General Assembly adopted General Assembly Resolution 181 recommending Israel's independence from British mandate. In 1948 the United Nations declared it to be the State of Israel. That same year Israel was invaded by several of its Arab neighbors: Egypt, Jordan, Syria and some forces from Iraq. The war lasted 10 months and Israel prevailed. Israel was again attacked in 1967 by Egypt, Jordan, and Syria. This time the war only lasted six days and Israel again prevailed. I'm trying not to sound bigoted here but those Arabs seem to be shortsighted and slow learners. Israel maintained control of some of the territory it captured in an effort to prevent future invasions from those areas. Israel kept control of the Sinai Peninsula and the Gaza Strip from Egypt; East Jerusalem and the West Bank from Jordan; the Golan Heights from Syria. Israel withdrew its forces from the Sinai Peninsula in 1977 under an agreement that neither Egypt nor Israel would put military forces on the ground in that area. In 2011 Egypt sent military forces back into the Sinai which effectively broke the 1977 agreement. Israel gave up control of the Gaza Strip to the Palestinian Authority in 1993 and completely withdrew in 2005. Israelis are in East Jerusalem and the West Bank to this day. They are under constant international pressure, including from the United States, to leave that territory.

Let's clear up a few facts about how the so-called Palestinian refugees ended up in refugee camps. Prior to the 1967 Arab invasion the Arabs living in Israeli territory were warned to leave by the invaders so they would not be caught up in the massacre of the Jews. The Jews did not force them out. After the Arab invaders were summarily spanked by Israel the Arab refugees refused to return. They were not denied re-entry into Israel by the Israelis. They have maintained they are victims at the hands of the Israelis and have used that victim status to garner sympathy on the world stage; not to mention very large sums of money.

Israel, and to a lesser degree Jordan, is the only true ally the United States has in that entire region. But the sad truth is Mr. Obama and the people he surrounds himself with, and specifically the US State Department under his leadership, have systematically and intentionally disrespected Israel and its leaders. Mr. Obama's allegiance to the Arab world has become painfully clear judging by the way he has personally treated Israel and President Netanyahu and the way he has personally treated the regions dictators, bullies, and kings. Could the US Secretary of State, John Kerry, have been more offensive to Israel than by saying they are on the path to becoming an apartheid state if they don't give in to Palestinian demands? I am going to give Mr. Kerry the benefit of the doubt and assume he is simply ignorant of the meaning of apartheid. If Mr. Kerry does know the meaning of apartheid, then he has offended a very important ally. In either case, he needs to find a new line of work. He would fit in nicely as a Beltway lobbyist for the Iranian mullahs.

I've never understood why US administrations and their diplomats feel they have the right to dictate Israeli policy. Just because the US government throws Israel a few taxpayer dollars, doesn't give it the right to tell Israel how to handle it own affairs. The US government gives billions of taxpayer dollars each year to the Palestinian Authority, does that not give them the right to tell the Palestinian Authority they must accept the existence of Israel? But instead, the United States gives military supplies and US taxpayer cash to the Palestinian Authority, who then gives those supplies and US taxpayer cash to Hamas and the al-Aqsa Martyrs Brigade, who then use those American supplies and US taxpayer cash to kill Jewish citizens. I guess in a roundabout way the United States taxpayer is guilty of killing Jewish people. Don't you think that should stop?

Judging by their past, American liberals have never met a dictator or thug they don't admire and support. They envy the power and control the dictator has over his people because that is the type of absolute power and control the liberals would like to have over the American people. Sending these pathetic Arab dictators and their anti-Semite neighbors billions upon billions of US taxpayer dollars has allowed the thugs to remain in power. The United States should abandon our military and financial support of those petty tyrants and resume a solid relationship with our only democratically ruled, Middle Eastern ally, Israel. This little tirade brings to mind a question I have always wanted to ask American Jewish voters:

"Keeping in mind the way liberals have treated you in the past and in the present, why do you still vote for Democrats?" It's one of those mysteries of the universe that will never have an answer.

There will never be an end to the Arab/Israeli conflict with a "two state solution". Does anyone honestly believe the Arabs will leave Israel alone if Israel gives them a few acres of sand and rocks? The Arabs single focus is the total destruction of the State of Israel and its occupants. As far as they are concerned that is the only solution to the conflict. I have always wanted to ask any Arab or any anti-Semite this question: "How would your life be different if Israel and the Jewish people had never existed?" I expect that would be a very difficult question for them to answer honestly. I believe that area of the world would still be virtually uninhabitable desert. There would be a few towns and settlements along the coast but the balance of the inland property would be devoid of human development. There would be no giant mosque and for that matter, no Jerusalem. Israel is not large, only 10,400 square miles, about the size of Massachusetts. South Israel is the Negev desert which occupies almost 6,200 square miles leaving only 4,200 square miles of inhabitable property. If the Israelis were to give up the West Bank at 2,300 square miles and the Golan Heights of 450 square miles that would only leave 1,475 square miles, an area smaller than Rhode Island. If Israel were forced to give up the West Bank and Golan Heights it might be a little crowded in Israel with a population of almost 8 million. Rhode Island has a population of just over 1 million.

As I pointed out previously, Israel is as legitimate and sovereign a nation as any other in the region. It's established boundaries are the result of war and settlement. Thousands of years ago the Israelis settled on the sand and rock piles that now make up Israel. The only inhabitants there when the Israelis arrived were traders who crossed the region for the sole purpose of access to the open ocean. There is considerable archaeological evidence that the large domed mosques in Jerusalem are built on top of older Jewish structures. The land was so harsh no one wanted to settle on it, but it was the Promised Land given to them by God. Much of Israel is still uninhabited but the inhabited areas are lush fields and thriving communities. The only people responsible for the success of Israel are the Israelis themselves and the Arab-Israelis that have the common sense to live there. The way Arab-Israeli's are treated by the Israeli population is a testament to how other Arabs would be treated if the Israelis were given a chance. They live as neighbors, friends, family, and coworkers.

# TERRORISM *and* EXTREMISM

*"We cannot play innocents abroad in a world that is not innocent."*
Ronald Reagan

This is the Chapter where I earn the label "Islamaphobe". I'm going to cover some of the history of acts of terror committed against the United States for the last 35 years or so. It pretty much all started under President Jimmy Carter because he showed weakness to the Iranian mullahs. To show their appreciation for allowing them to take over Iran, in 1979 they kidnapped 66 hostages from our embassy in Tehran; 14 were released; the remaining 52 were kept in captivity for 444 days. The proof that they knew how weak Carter's leadership was but how strong America could be under a strong leader; they released the hostages the day Ronald Reagan was sworn in as president in 1981.

There were 20 attacks in the years 1979 through 1999. That was one attack per year. There have been 26 attacks in the years 2000 through 2014. The average has gone up by 70% per year. There is no indication under another weak president like Obama that that trend will not continue to spiral upward. To be fair, there were 13 attacks in the 8 years under Bush's watch. There have been 12 attacks in the 5 ½ years under Obama's watch. If you are doing the math: the 24th attack was in October 2000 against the USS Cole in a Yemeni port under Clinton's watch.

There were 10 attacks on US soil beginning with the first World Trade Center bombing in 1993. Three of the 10 attacks were perpetrated by insane Americans. The other 7 attacks were perpetrated by insane Muslims. Eighteen attacks were committed against US embassies, military bases, and one American warship. Ten attacks involved airliners, airports or cruise ships. The last 8 attacks were committed on civilian foreign soil like hotels and restaurants. The two common factors in all of the attacks were: the ultimate targets were Americans; virtually 100% of the perpetrators were Islamic terrorists. You can whine and cry and call me all the names you want but the facts are the facts. We can bow to all the Muslim dictators and kings around the world and it won't change the fact that they hate us and want us dead.

I limited this chapter's statistics to the terrorism of America because that is what hits home for me. But I would like to point out that there are thousands upon thousands of similar attacks by Muslim terrorists on civilians in virtually every country of the world. Christians are being murdered by the thousands and their churches destroyed all around the world. The idea that there are moderate Muslims appears to be a myth. If they are not doing the actual killing they are either financing the killers or enabling them by not speaking out against their actions.

I noticed while doing research for this chapter that the bulk of the terrorists involved in murdering Americans come from Saudi Arabia, Iran, Yemen, Lebanon, and Syria. Why do we continue to send money to these countries? Why do we still do business with these countries? Why are we even talking to these countries? Just a thought: if we were allowed to produce our own domestic oil we could stop funding our own destruction.

I saw a TV clip a few years back of a group of 100+ top Al Qaeda leaders that had gathered together for the funeral of a fellow terrorist. I don't recall if it was in Afghanistan or Iraq. I thought at the time what a wonderful opportunity the US wasted to take out a very large group of the terrorist leadership with a quick F-16 bombing run. Some would say that's not the way we do things in America but I'm here to say on some occasions it should be exactly the way we do things. This is an unconventional war with terrorism and unconventional methods need to be used to defeat it. We cannot fight by our rules of fair play while they play by their rules of no-holds-barred. It does not matter that we carry a bigger stick than them. It matters whether or not we are willing to use the entire stick or we "choke-up" on it before we whack them. I'm not recommending the use of nuclear weapons but we do need to have a philosophy of winning like we did with Japan to end World War II and stop the hundreds of thousands of additional deaths that would have occurred on both sides had the war continued.

# AMERICAN CIVIL LIBERTIES UNION

*"It is as useless to argue with those who have renounced the use of reason as to administer medication to the dead."*                    Thomas Jefferson

The ACLU never takes on conservative causes. Everything they do is based on their liberal/socialist agenda. The causes they champion are anti-religious, anti-gun, pro-abortion, pro-gay, anti-military, pro-terrorist, anti-American family, anti-American flag, and just anti-American in general. They cringe when they hear of a third grade class citing the Pledge of Allegiance or a high school sports team huddling for prayer before and after a game. Just talking about a 10 Commandments monument on the lawn of a courthouse in flyover country gives them cold chills. In their world, socialist ideology dictates the agenda to be followed. Roger Baldwin, the founder of the ACLU, was a devout socialist with communist leanings but disavowed communism in the 1940s after witnessing communist rule in the old Soviet Union under Joseph Stalin's regime. I can't imagine he remained a supporter of socialist causes when socialism is only one short step above communism. As the founder of the ACLU Mr. Baldwin is undoubtedly an atheist. At least we won't have to encounter him in heaven.

The bulk of the funding for the ACLU comes from liberal/socialist nonprofit organizations, membership dues, and individual donors like George Soros, a world renowned socialist, felon billionaire. The taxpayers of many states inadvertently provide funding to the ACLU in the form of court awarded dollars when the ACLU sues their state or school system and the ACLU wins. The ACLU does lose some cases and has to pay their opponents attorney fees, but that seldom happens. They normally win, even if they don't have legitimate standing to pursue a case in court, just by threatening and terrorizing an individual or entity with a lawsuit. If you stand up to them they can be beat. There are many legal-based groups in the United States that would be more than glad to take on the ACLU. Entities are finding out that if they stand firm and even push back the ACLU will slink away to find a less aggressive target to force their socialist agenda on.

There are provisions in the US civil liberties laws that allow the ACLU to sue a government entity and if the ACLU wins they collect attorneys fees and expert witness fees accrued over the course of that case. Those fees are awarded at the discretion of the sitting judge so you know the ACLU makes every effort to file cases in liberal-leaning, sympathetic judge's courts. It makes sense that the winner can collect those fees. The problem for the American taxpayer is that the government entity can't collect those same fees in their behalf even if they win. In other words, taxpayers pay the ACLU to sue them. Is the American court system great or what? The generosity of the American taxpayer knows no bounds.

# RACISM *and* BIGOTRY

*"The foundation on which our Constitution was built is the natural equality of man."*
                                                                    Thomas Jefferson

**Racist:** *"a person who advocates for or believes in the superiority or inferiority of a particular group on the basis of supposed racial differences".*

**Bigot:** *"one whose attitude or behavior expresses intolerance because of race, religion, politics, etc".*

If you accept those two definitions then you have to accept the fact that every person on the planet is a racist and/or a bigot. What race of people doesn't believe their race is superior to any other? What religion doesn't believe their religion is better than any other? What political affiliation doesn't believe their ideology is not superior to any other? Anyone who calls another person a racist or bigot is a hypocrite because he/she is one or both themselves. Racist is without a doubt the most misused word in America. Liberals have hijacked the word to prevent Republicans from speaking. A liberal pundit a while back claimed using the word "Chicago" was racist because that is where Obama is from. Republicans are called racists any time they make any mention of Obama's policies or ideologies. Using that logic, Obama is a racist for his never-ending criticism of George Bush and his policies. I know, using logic and common sense with a liberal is like talking to your neighbor's fence. Republicans were called racists when they mentioned that Black Panthers carrying weapons in front of a public polling precinct was illegal. Republicans were called racists when they were upset that Attorney General Eric Holder refused to arrest and prosecute those same Black Panthers. Americans are called racists when they feel that illegal immigrants should be arrested and returned to their own country. Americans are called racists and bigots when they ask the American government to profile airline travelers from specific countries in an effort to make Americans safer. There is no safety or security in a country that has allowed political correctness to rule it's every thought and action. It has reached a so-called fever pitch and hopefully true Americans will stand up and be heard in our upcoming 2014 and 2016 elections.

Liberals have usurped the words racist and bigot. They have limited the meaning specifically to white conservative men. They claim that white men having power over minorities of color is now the new meaning of racist. The fact is, whether you accept it or not, white conservative men

93

have nearly zero power over minorities. There are so many guardians over minority status that white conservative men aren't even allowed to discuss race in public. In fact, as Donald Sterling, the owner of the Los Angeles Clippers basketball team learned, you can't even talk about race in private. My take on Mr. Sterling is he is a complete jackass and that description probably goes beyond his racist leanings. He is the liberal's new devil incarnate. While on that topic let me ask a question: is Larry Johnson, an ex-Knicks player a racist for advocating for an all-black basketball league?

Liberals are only outraged when Republicans say or do what they consider to be racist but are not outraged when their own say or do the same type of things. No one was outraged when Hillary, on the 2008 presidential campaign trail, used a condescending, stereotypical "plantation dialect" to ingratiate herself to black voters. No one was outraged when Harry Reid suggested that Obama was capable of using the "Negro Dialect" when it was to Obama's advantage to do so. No one cried "racist" when crazy Uncle Joe Biden said Obama is a clean, articulate black presidential candidate. Was he inferring that past black presidential candidates Jesse Jackson and Al Sharpton were dirty and illiterate? Everyone just chuckled when crazy Uncle Joe made the comment you "cannot go to a 7-Eleven or a Dunkin Doughnuts without a slight India accent". No liberals were outraged over the fact that Democratic Senator Robert Byrd was at one time a recruiter for the KKK; nor when he used the term white nig..r on national television twice in 2001. No liberal was outraged when Clarence Thomas was called an "Uncle Tom" during his US Supreme Court nomination and several more times since being seated on the bench. No liberals were outraged when Condoleezza Rice was depicted as George Bush's parrot in a very distasteful cartoon caricature. Blacks affectionately call each other the N-word on a regular basis which negates its racial tone. The N-word is only a racist word when white Republicans use it? What is left of American politics when we are no longer allowed to be critical of a sitting president's failed policies regardless of his skin color? No white Republican president was ever awarded that courtesy.

I'm here to say that racism cuts in all directions. If you accept the above definition of racism literally then no one is immune from it and no one is innocent of it. With that in mind, and the fact that liberals believe you are racist if you have more power than someone of a different race, I have put together a list of non-white individuals and organizations that are more powerful than I and are therefore racist: Al Sharpton; Barack Obama; Michelle Obama; Jeremiah Wright; Jesse Jackson; La Raza; Snoopy Doggy

Dog; Black Panthers; Spike Lee; Van Jones; Harry Belafonte; Congressional Black Caucus; NAACP; Council on American-Islamic Relations; Frank Marshall Davis; and last but not least, Hank Aaron for calling Obama's critics KKK in "neckties and starched shirts".

I am going to pose some questions with no expectations that they would ever receive a legitimate answer from the left. What would happen if colleges around the country were allowed to set up white student unions in response to black student unions? What would happen if white politicians set up a Congressional White Caucus in response to the Congressional Black Caucus? What would happen if Christians in the United States started killing Muslims and burning their mosques in response to the Muslims doing the same to Christians all around the world? What would be the response if Americans infiltrated Mexico's northern border in the same fashion and numbers that Mexicans infiltrate our southern border? Would Americans get the same welcome if they floated over to Cuba as Cubans get when they float over to America? Would blacks have been slaves in America if their own tribesmen had not sold them into slavery? What would be the plight of American blacks if the liberals in the South had won the Civil War? What would the United States be called and what would it look like if the pilgrims had not landed on its eastern shores nearly 400 years ago? I'll answer the last part of that last question: All of the above questions would be moot. None of it would have ever happened; good, bad or indifferent, if the white Christians had never come to America.

Race baiting is the bread-and-butter of the liberal party in general and many individuals specifically. They keep minorities of color under their control by erroneously pretending to protect them from the evil racists and bigots. The fact is the race baiters are all racists themselves due to the fact that they have purposely convinced their followers that they don't have the wherewithal to take care of themselves. "Nanny State" at its finest! Individuals such as Jesse Jackson, Al Sharpton, Louis Farrakhan, Jeremiah Wright, and many others have made themselves very comfortable livings on the backs of fellow minorities. If the race baiters didn't continue to keep racism and bigotry at a boiling point American society would eventually heal itself and they would need to find a legitimate line of work. Stop listening to them and get on with life. Embrace the truth about America: there is no better place on earth to live.

I don't know about anyone else but I'm really tired of being called a racist and bigot just because of the color of my skin. You don't know what's in my heart. So if you're judging me based on the color of my skin you,

95

my friend, are a racist. Saying I'm tired of being held responsible for what happened over 150 years ago is not racism on my part, it's anger. I'm angry about being held responsible for what happened in America before my ancestors arrived here. The racists that say I'm responsible for 150 years ago are the same people who don't hold Obama responsible for what he did yesterday. Stop listening to the race baiters call you victims. Slavery ended 150 years ago at a cost of 360,000 white Union soldiers' lives; America elected a black president – twice; that doesn't sound racist to me.

# DEATH PENALTY

*"We must reject the idea that every time a law's broken, society is guilty rather than the lawbreaker. It is time to restore the American precept that each individual is accountable for his actions."*                Ronald Reagan

I was living in Florida in 1989 when Ted Bundy was executed for the rape and murder of a 12-year-old girl. He had committed dozens of similar murders over the complete width of the United States. Five hundred people outside the penitentiary in Stark, Florida cheered when Ted Bundy was electrocuted for his crimes. That is no longer the case. Crowds that gather at executions now hold vigils in behalf of the murderer and not the victims. I recall at the time the "bleeding heart" arguments against the death penalty: it is barbaric to kill another human being; it cost $2 million to execute a man and only $50,000 per year to keep him in prison; the death penalty is not a deterrent to the commission of capital crime. All those arguments, plus the argument that death is a cruel and unusual punishment, are as applicable today as they were in 1989. All those arguments are specious. Each argument on its own is plausible but wrong. It implies that it was okay for Bundy to kill young girls but not for the criminal justice system to kill Bundy. Bundy was executed with 2,000 volts of electricity that lasted only one minute. The cost of the electricity couldn't have been more than $.50. As for the costs of the officers involved in setting up the execution and the executioner pushing the button, virtually all of the parents and siblings of his victims would have pushed that button for free. The Florida penitentiary system could have made money by having an open bid for who got to push the button. And last but not least, the reason that the death penalty is not a deterrent is because the average length of time between sentencing and execution in 2012 was nearly 16 years. That is the average number of years on death row but it's not unusual for an inmate to be on death row for 20 years or more. Gary Alvord was on death row in Florida for 40 years and died in prison in 2013 of natural causes. But the main reason the death penalty is not a deterrent is because in 2009 only 1.64% of inmates sentenced to death were actually executed. They receive pardons or their sentences are commuted to life in prison or some other outcome that saves their worthless lives.

Death row inmates are no longer regarded by many people as the cowardly human garbage that they truly are. In the minds of many people, especially the majority of liberals, the murderers have become the victims.

There is no regard given for the real victim or the victim's families. It is hard to comprehend how that complete reversal has taken place. I find it particularly ironic that the liberals who call the death penalty cruel and unusual punishment are the same liberals who have sanctioned the murder of over 50 million babies by abortion.

The predominantly used method of execution in the United States is lethal injection using three drugs: the first drug injected is an anesthetic that deadens any pain; the second drug used is a paralytic that will prevent the inmate from speaking and skeletal muscles from spasming; the last drug used is potassium chloride which stops the heart. It all sounds pretty painless to me. My preferred method of judgment would be to inflict the same manner of death on the inmate as was inflicted on the victim(s). If there was torture and/or rape those would also be inflicted on the inmate for the same length of time that the victim had to endure it.

I have a few ideas that should alleviate many concerns about the cruel and unusual aspect of the death penalty that the liberals tout as a reason to discontinue its use. I made these up on my own; I am parroting liberal ideology in the application of these death penalty techniques. First of all, you may recall the death of Terri Schiavo in Florida in 2005. She was in a coma and kept alive for 15 years with a feeding tube. Terri's husband Michael, for reasons known only to him, Terri, and God initiated and won a court case which allowed him to have the feeding tube removed. She lasted nearly 14 days after the tube was removed. Because George Bush intervened on behalf of Terri's parents, who were opposed to letting Terri die, the liberals were in favor of letting her die. We were told that she felt no pain and would die a peaceful death by starvation. What liberal could now be opposed to allowing death row inmates be starved and die a peaceful death? Forget the horrific deaths by lethal injection that takes a mere five minutes rather than two weeks. Another method to be considered would be the use of "green" electricity for execution. The prison warden would have to certify that the electricity used for the prisoner's execution came from a renewable source such as water or wind turbine or a Chinese owned solar array located in the Nevada desert. What better last tribute could be heaped upon a mass murderer by his liberal camp-followers? If the state uses a firing squad then the warden would have to certify the bullets used are lead-free. If the state uses hanging to carry out their death sentence they would be required to use hemp rope rather than nylon rope because nylon is made from evil fossil fuel. By virtue of using the hemp rope the final tribute could be all of the murder's sympathizers sit around the campfire singing "Cumbaya" and smoking the rope. The last suggestion that should be readily acceptable to liberals is to conform to Islam, the "religion of peace", and apply the Sharia law of death by stoning. Would that not make it a peaceful death?

I don't particularly care what method is used to enforce the death penalty. The only thing that should matter is that it is inevitable and swift once a judge and jury deem it appropriate. Many years of appeals and delays would be ended. If the evidence and witnesses are irrefutable, 60 days should be time sufficient for the death row inmate to prepare to meet his maker. Swift and sure application of the death penalty would then truly be a deterrent to capital murder. If you applied my preferred method of judgment (die the way you killed) the murder rate would drop to negligible numbers immediately upon conclusion of the first death sentence.

# DRUG WARS

*"Let us not forget who we are. Drug abuse is a repudiation of everything America is."*
Ronald Reagan

Richard Nixon declared his "war on drugs" in 1971 but Ronald Reagan began a serious law enforcement campaign against drugs in the early 80s. In 1980 there were approximately 50,000 individuals in American prisons for drug law crimes. Less than forty years later, and about $1 trillion spent, we have 500,000 individuals in prison for drug law crimes. With those two statistics it is still hard to tell if we are winning or losing the war. Are we winning because we have 500,000 people off the streets that were involved in drug law crimes? Or are we losing because we're spending resources that could be used in the pursuit of criminals who have committed much more heinous crimes? I don't have answers for those questions but one thing I'm pretty sure of: decriminalizing the use of drugs is not the answer.

It will be nearly impossible to stop the legalization of drugs now that Colorado and Washington have legalized marijuana and Colorado is predicting revenues to the state to be around $100 million in 2014. It will be hard for other cash-strapped states to ignore that giant "cash cow" that looms large with the legalization of marijuana. Hopefully they will wait a few years to see what the consequences are for Colorado and Washington before jumping on the "Mary Jane Revenue Bandwagon". But, alas, that is not the way greedy politicians think.

Colorado has a 10% retail sales tax on marijuana and a 15% sales tax at the wholesale level. If it is taxed 15% when the grower sells it and additional 10% when the retail shop sells it, then Colorado is collecting 25% on each dollar of marijuana sales. If the State taxes it too heavily they will price the legal retailers out of the market and the guy on the street corner will again be the go-to-man for the dope buyers. That will probably be the case because the greedy government types cannot help themselves when they come across an open trough full of cash.

I will admit that someone put a considerable amount of time into setting up the legal hoops to jump through in order to become a marijuana seller or cultivator in Colorado. Go to the Colorado Department of Revenue, Division of Taxation, and look up "Information for Cultivators". That's some pretty intense legalese. I would not recommend trying to read the statutory requirements if you have recently partaken of a sample of the subject matter in question.

Many argued that the Prohibition Act in effect in the 1920s that made alcohol sales illegal wasn't effective because all it did was create a bootleg industry and the lawlessness that came with the black market sale of booze. Armed with that argument the legalizers say all criminal activity surrounding marijuana sales will cease once the drugs are legalized. I say there is no way for anyone to accurately predict what affects there will be with newly legalized drugs. Having said that, I'm going to make a few predictions. I predict the drug cartels are not going to take kindly to such a large encroachment into their business so legal growers and legal sellers may be in for some nasty surprises from the bad boys. I predict use of marijuana will increase because of the decrease of fear of incarceration and the stigma of being a pothead. There will not be a decrease in the personal dependency of a drug just because you made it legal. Personal dependence on alcohol did not decrease after Prohibition was repealed in 1933.

Negative unintended consequences seem to always pop up shortly after some harebrained liberal legislation is passed into law. The law passed in November 2012. Early in 2013 the liberal legislators in Colorado got the news that teenage use of marijuana had increased and they were scratching their heads wondering why that happened!

Legalizing marijuana in Colorado did open up another revenue stream beyond the millions in taxes. Colorado has now instituted a new revenue producing program called "Drive High - Get DUI". The benefits from legalizing marijuana may never end!

There are studies that claim marijuana is a "gateway" drug to other more dangerous drugs. I know people who would stand in line for days for the opportunity to be in those studies. There are an equal number of studies that refute that claim. As a non-user of any illegal drugs I cannot vouch for either argument. The crowd that supports the use of marijuana by using the argument "it is no worse than alcohol" conveniently forgets the fact that the use of alcohol is legal. I am not in the business of judging people based on a physical or mental addiction to illicit drugs. I will say it is sad that so many millions of Americans have had their lives destroyed by the poison sold on the street corners all across America. I also hope there is an especially nasty place in hell for the people that provide that poison to our children.

Speaking of children I will switch gears to a much lighter topic. There was a story that came out of Colorado about a young Girl Scout who set up her cookie sales table on the sidewalk in front of a marijuana shop. I don't know what the rest of you think, but I believe that young lady has a very bright future. Even though the State of Colorado legalized marijuana for the tax revenue, city officials decided that this young lady, who was also in pursuit of revenue, was not allowed to sell munchies to the potheads who exited the store. She had to move her cookie sales table from in front of the store. This is another example of liberals telling America "to do as we say and not as we do".

I heard recently that the National Football League is considering relaxing its pot rules for players. When I heard that, the first thing that popped into my unprepossessing mind was the sideline scene in Mash (the movie) where the players on the bench were passing a joint. I readily admit that I am easily amused. (Unprepossessing: not overtly impressive; unremarkable; nondescript.)

# INTRUSIVE GOVERNMENT

*"My reading of history convinces me that most bad government results from too much government."* Thomas Jefferson

*"Experience hath shown that even under the best forms of government those entrusted with power have, in time, and by slow operations, perverted it into tyranny."* Thomas Jefferson

*"If people let government decide what foods they drink and what medicines they take, their bodies will soon be in as sorry a state as are the souls of those who live under tyranny."* Thomas Jefferson

The American governmental systems at all levels from city, county, state, and federal have completely lost all regard for the American Constitution as designed by our Founding Fathers. The Declaration of Independence, the US Constitution, and the Bill of Rights were designed to limit government and highlight the rights of American citizens to be protected from their own overreaching federal government. The governmental system during the course of this great nation has completely reversed that concept. The American people were specifically given "unalienable rights" by their Creator to "Life, Liberty and Pursuit of Happiness". Under our current system of government we no longer control our lives; our liberties are quickly disintegrating; and happiness is becoming a thing of the past.

The people in control of the three branches of government, the Executive, Legislative, and Judicial have become so like-minded that they are no longer the watchdogs of each other's antics as designated by the U.S. Constitution. To them "we the people" have become the enemy. What has become the primary goal of all elected officials, agency heads, and pretty much all civil servants in general is to remain in power and control every aspect of the American population's lives. We have become so taxed, regulated, intimidated, and dependant on and by our governmental system we have to ask for the blessing to live from our very own employees. Our Founding Fathers put in print, on purpose, the very things that the federal government is limited in doing: national defense and protecting our sovereignty from both foreign and domestic enemies. Over the years our elected officials, with the aid of the judicial system, have literally pulled nonexistent governmental rights out of the blue sky. It has taken collusion, conspiracy, and some very creative forms of corruption on their part to get us into our present Constitutional calamity.

Something that should alarm every American citizen is the fact that all levels of domestic government, from local to federal, are developing military tactical training, obtaining military weaponry, and hoarding ammunition. I see no other purpose for this than preparing to enforce domestic policies on the American population at gunpoint. I would love to hear some other plausible reason. Can someone explain to me why the Environmental Protection Agency sends a SWAT team to knock down your door if you accidentally kill a burrowing owl on your own vacant lot? Can someone explain to me why the Internal Revenue Service sends a SWAT team to your office to collect your financial files for a tax evasion investigation? Can anyone tell me why Homeland Security has bought up billions of rounds of ammunition? They claim it is practice ammunition. The truth is they are purchasing "people killer" ammunition and enough of it to accommodate a couple hundred years of practice. These are all domestic agencies and not one of them goes overseas and participates in fighting a foreign enemy. Why would they possibly need to militarize their agencies? It has become abundantly clear to me that the purpose for all of this is our domestic agencies are preparing to declare war on the American population. We are the enemy. I have never been a big conspiracy theorist but things are changing quickly. There are too many facts that add up to pending calamities. Don't ignore the facts; prepare yourselves; the government is.

I have always known that our federal government system was massive but I didn't realize how massive until I started doing research for this book. I'm going to give you an idea of how large it is with some very interesting numbers. In September 2013 there were in excess of 2.7 million civilians in the employ of the US taxpayers. That does not include our elected officials and our military personnel. The 2.7 million are spread out over an enormous array of federal civil servant positions.

Mr. Obama and Crazy Uncle Joe's Executive branch includes large staffs and offices for each of them and Obama's 38 "czars". The Legislative branch includes large staffs and offices for 100 Senators and 435 members of the House of Representatives. The Judicial branch consists of the Supreme Court with its offices and staff for each of the 9 US Supreme Court justices; below them would be the 13 US Circuit Courts of Appeal with their offices and staffs; below them are the 94 US District Courts with their offices and staff. Currently there are approximately 3,600 federal judges employed by the American taxpayers.

There are 15 federal "Departments of" consisting of Agriculture, Commerce, Defense, Education, Energy, Health and Human Services, Homeland Security, Housing and Urban Development, Interior, Justice, Labor, State, Transportation, Treasury, and Veterans Administration. Within these 15 Departments there are 313 agencies or bureaus. There are 161 sub agencies or bureaus. There are 21 sub/sub agencies or bureaus. That is the part of the federal government that directly employs the 2.7 million civil servants. There are nearly 200 additional agencies, boards, commissions, bureaus, and corporations that are at least partially government-owned and/or are supported by taxpayer funds. Now you know why American taxpayers own 900,000 buildings. Is it any wonder most American people consider our federal bureaucracy bloated to the extent of wasteful and should be reduced in size?

With the exception of the Department of State and the Department of Defense the sole reason for the existence of every department, agency, bureau, and "office of" is to regulate, enforce, and punish the American population. Not a single one of these agencies was designed to regulate the federal government itself even though the U.S. Constitution was very specific concerning that very thing. Elitist federal bureaucracy members have no interest in policing themselves but exist and thrive on policing "we the people".

The patients are running the insane asylum and "we the people" are the doctors that are tasked to come up with a remedy to that situation. It is way beyond time to lighten the taxpayer's load by eliminating some of the redundant agencies. The American people have had to tighten their financial belts; the federal government needs to do the same. The only way we can do that is to elect and send like-minded people to Washington and hope they can stand up to the flack they will be receiving from the firmly ensconced Washington brethren.

*"No government ever voluntarily reduces itself in size. Government programs, once launched, never disappear. Actually, a government bureau is the nearest thing to eternal life we'll ever see on this earth!"* Ronald Reagan

# EMMINENT DOMAIN

*"Whenever there are in any country uncultivated lands and unemployed poor, it is clear that the laws of property have been so far extended as to violate natural right. The earth is given as a common stock for man to labor and live on. The small landowners are the most precious part of a state."*

Thomas Jefferson

I'm not going to go into depth about this topic. I just want everyone to know how widespread and detrimental to property rights/ownership this government policy has become. In the past, government at all levels would use eminent domain to take private land for public use. The eminent domain statutes normally have verbiage that states the government can take private property for a beneficial public use and for many years that was pretty much limited to public roads and schools and not much else. The problem with that verbiage is that it has been interpreted, even at the US Supreme Court level, to mean the government can take private land for any use the government deems beneficial. Cities and counties around the country have been taking private property with occupied homes and giving it to groups of private developers. The developers purchase the confiscated property from the government at lower than market values and build high-rise residences, businesses, and higher revenue producing buildings than the single family homes produced. Higher tax revenues to the city are considered to be a beneficial public use. A lot of these properties are well located on waterfront or near water making them extremely valuable. Many of the owners will refuse to sell because they are offered considerably less money than the actual value of their property. Others refuse to sell because the properties have been in their families for generations. Those things do not matter to the government entity because they know they can force the owners to settle for whatever funds the government offers. With the possible exceptions of the IRS confiscation of private property in lieu of taxes and law enforcement confiscation of private property at drug busts, eminent domain is without a doubt the most egregious form of government greed in the US. I have an idea, why doesn't a group of homeowners go to their local government and say "We have waterfront property to develop and we want you to confiscate private cash from some rich individuals so we have the means to develop the property". Explain to me the difference between having the cash to develop and needing a property, or having property to develop and needing the cash. Kind of puts a new spin on eminent domain!

The Supreme Court case that blew the lid off containment of government confiscation of private property was called Kelo vs. City of New London. In 2005 the US Supreme Court ruled 5-4 to allow the city of New London, Connecticut to condemn an entire neighborhood and bulldoze all the homes to make way for private development. After the homes were bulldozed the developer backed out of the deal. Now nine years later the property that was a thriving residential neighborhood is now an overgrown vacant wasteland. It didn't turn out the way the city officials of New London or the five justices in the Supreme Court had envisioned. The city owns the property. They spent a considerable amount of money demolishing and hauling off the original homes. All the property is off the tax rolls and has not produced property tax revenue for nine years. With the economy currently in the toilet it doesn't look like it will be revenue-producing property again anytime soon. Government bureaucracy at its finest.

# JOBS *and* UNEMPLOYMENT

*"Recession is when a neighbor loses his job. Depression is when you lose yours."*
Ronald Reagan

Over the years Americans have been the most employed people in the world. We have worked the hardest, the smartest, the longest hours, all with the least amount of vacation time compared to most workers around the world. For many years possessing a job was based on you being the best person for that particular job. Pay scales were determined by position and merit. The better you were at a job the more likely you were to receive advancement and additional pay. If an employer didn't pay you what you felt you deserved you found a job that did. American workers, for several decades, have been very mobile and found it easy to obtain a better job down the street or across the country. With the employment situation we find ourselves in presently, the American worker is more apt to stay in a job he doesn't like.

The free market should always determine wages and benefits. With interference from the government and the use of strikes and collective bargaining by unions all of that has gone down the toilet. Many employers are no longer allowed to pay employees based on their skill level or productivity. Owners and upper-level management have become the managed. The workers have secured the ability to set their own wages and benefit packages. Of course there were employer abuses as well. In the past an employer could fire anyone for any cause. In the present if the business owner wants to fire even a nonproductive worker, that owner better be prepared to pay unemployment compensation for the next 96 weeks. If the reason for termination hasn't been properly logged in an employee file there's also a good chance of being sued and having to pay back-pay from termination date.

I'm going to allow the sexist in me to rear its ugly head for a couple comments. The priorities of many women have changed considerably over the last few decades. Many chose career over marriage and family and that was perfectly fine for them. But in the past marriage and motherhood was a career. Employment was merely a means to supplement the household income or just get out of the house a few hours each day. Women, compared to men who were viewed as the "breadwinners", tended to want to work fewer hours and except less responsibility. Women have always asked for more time off, for vital reasons such as nurturing and caring for children and family members. Men tended to be more accepting of moving to a different company location to advance their careers. Men can do heavier lifting. Women tend to be more emotional in their decision-making. All of the above have historically contributed to lower wage scales for women. But times have changed. Some of the toughest and most successful business managers around the world are women. Ladies, I sincerely hope the "equal pay for equal work" campaign works out for you. Just remember, you control half the money and half the votes in America!

In January 2004 the unemployment rate was 5.7%. It trended slowly down for the next 4 ½ years to reach a low of 5% in April 2008. It then started back up and was at 5.8% at the end of 2008. It reached a peak of 10% in October 2009. November 2009 through most of 2010 it stayed in the high 9s. Mr. Bush's negative influence began to subside in January 2011 when unemployment began slowly declining to reach 6.3% in April 2014. Kudos to Mr. Obama for producing so many jobs for Americans. I find it amusing that everything wrong with America to this day is still blamed on George Bush by the current administration. The exception to that rule is that Mr. Obama has single-handedly lowered the unemployment rate.

Unemployment numbers are easily manipulated. We have to believe whatever the administration tells us is true. Unemployment rates are based on what is called the "Labor Participation Rate". What that refers to is the number of people who are employed or who are currently seeking employment. When you give up looking for a job, or your unemployment benefits run out, you are no longer counted as unemployed. There have been millions of Americans who have done just that which lowers the number of unemployed which in turn lowers the percentage of unemployed. That is how the liberals claim the unemployment rate to be so low. I'll use easy numbers to illustrate: there were 100 people with jobs; 10 people lost their jobs; that is an unemployment rate of 10%; of the 10 people unemployed 5 continue to look for work and 5 give up looking; with only 5 people continually looking for work and 100 available jobs the unemployment rate magically becomes 5%. In other words, be very skeptical of the Department of Labor Statistics numbers being pushed on us by the liberals.

I find it very hard to believe that there are hundreds of thousands of new jobs produced in America each month, but that is what the Obama administration tells us. If you believe that then you should also believe that the bulk of those jobs are part-time and unskilled positions being filled to a great degree by lower education and lower skilled employees. How else would you explain the high unemployment numbers of high school and college graduates? And I am making an assumption here that our current high school and college graduates are literate and highly skilled. There are a lot of educational statistics that belie that assumption.

I'll close this chapter with a couple of statistics from 2009: According to the U.S. Bureau of Economic Analysis, public employees received in excess of $123,000 in salaries and benefits compared to $61,000 for private sector employees. Pretty sad when the boss makes less than the employee.

# MINIMUM WAGE

*"Increasing the minimum wage is a bad move economically, philosophically and politically. The bottom line is we view it as an imposition of higher labor costs on businesses, particularly small businesses."*     Marc Freedman

*"The concept of minimum wage is crazy, if you really stop to think about it. If eight dollars an hour seems right, why not $20 an hour? If it's coming by order of the government, why stop at any level? Why not just say everyone should get what Gates gets?"*     Malcolm Wallop

What I assume Mr. Wallop means is that the government can set the minimum wage at any level they want because they don't have to pay it. The business owner pays it then passes the additional labor costs on in the form of price increases to the very consumers that just received the raise. Price increases wipe out wage increases. At any rate, the whole process of raising the minimum wage makes the government people feel better about themselves at the expense of the American taxpayer.

As is the case with most government schemes, minimum wage has morphed into something other than what it was originally designed to do. Minimum wage was originally designed to prevent businesses from taking advantage of their young summer help. Students on summer vacation from school, evening and weekend jobs during school, were given employment opportunities to make a little spending cash and begin the process of honing their work ethic and skills. Menial jobs at fast food restaurants, mom-and-pop grocery stores, convenience stores, car washes, and similar labor positions were typically given to teenagers. Over the years as our public education system has increasingly failed our high school graduates these low skilled, part-time jobs have become a way of life for many. It is a sad indictment of America's schools but it is a fact. More and more high school graduates are being added to the employment rolls without the skills to allow them to do even menial tasks. Many can't speak properly, many can't read, many can't write, and even more have no math skills whatsoever. None of those are advantages for a sales job that requires talking to customers and running a cash register.

Entry-level jobs and the pay scales accompanying them were never designed to cater to the financial needs of a head of household. Those jobs were never intended to be permanent employment for anyone. If a business owner is required to pay his least skilled employees high wages he will not employ a person for that task, he will increase the work load on the high wage employees already in his employment. He can't raise his prices enough to cover the additional employee costs and stay competitive. The talk of increasing minimum wage to $15 an hour is ridiculous. If an employer has two employees at $8 an hour he is going to eliminate one of those positions and make the surviving employee do twice the work. Higher minimum wage, regardless of what the liberals say, is a job killer. The Congressional Budget Office says the boost to $15 per hour minimum wage will cost 500,000 jobs by 2016. These guys are not supposed to pick sides so you have to assume their assessment is correct.

I can see a change not only with decreased employment numbers but also a decrease in the service provided to consumers. For instance, if a restaurant can't afford to hire additional help, the restaurant may discontinue service at the tables. Without wait staff and busboys the customer will have to order at the counter, dispose of his own trash, and pay his bill at a cash register rather than from the table. Goodbye Applebee's and hello Burger King. Liberals would actually be okay with that because then they wouldn't be required to leave a tip at the table.

Americans that are currently working at a minimum wage job have my respect. For them to continue to work at that pay scale speaks volumes about their personal integrity. Even though the American social welfare system would pay them three times more to sit on their butts on the couch at home and do nothing they still have enough self respect to continue to work. It speaks volumes for the many Americans with those jobs who would rather have a $20,000 a year job and receive a paycheck than have someone else give it to them. My hat is off to them. The current push by the liberals to increase the minimum wage has nothing to do with what they are calling a "living wage". With midterm elections coming up in just a few months their motives are transparent: 1. to buy votes; 2. to bash Republicans who oppose it. Wow, there really is some transparency in this liberal government after all!

# CIVIL RIGHTS

*"Protecting the rights of even the least individual among us is basically the only excuse the government has for even existing."*　　　　　Ronald Reagan

The Civil Rights Amendment of 1964 forbade discrimination by employers on the basis of sex or race in hiring and firing employees. The original bill was under consideration with race the only topic in an effort to stop discrimination against blacks in the workplace. Sex wording was added at the end but was not the last change. Section 703(a) of the amendment ultimately legislated: it was unlawful to "fail or refuse to hire or to discharge any individual, or otherwise to discriminate against any individual with respect to his compensation, terms, conditions or privileges or employment, because of such individual's race, color, religion, sex, or national origin". The legislative umbrella soon encompassed age and disability. This legislation was done with good intentions and for all the right reasons. President John Kennedy started the ball rolling in 1963 and after his death President Lyndon Johnson continued the effort to push through the legislation. What liberals don't want you to know is that a very large contingent of Democratic senators vigorously opposed the Civil Rights Amendment. Liberal icons such as Mike Mansfield, Richard Russell, Strom Thurmond, Al Gore Sr., and J. William Fulbright maintained a 54 day filibuster of the legislation which ended with Democrat Senator Robert Byrd's 14 hour closing talk. President Johnson's appeal to the Republicans for help passing the Civil Rights Amendment was answered. In the final vote 82% of the Senate Republicans voted for the legislation and only 66% of the Democrats. In the House, 80% of the Republicans voted for the legislation and only 63% of the Democrats. It is another of the liberal "inconvenient truths" that the civil rights legislation in 1964 would have failed at the hands of the Democrats if Lyndon Johnson had been unable to garner the Republican support. In the Senate, Robert Byrd of West Virginia was the only northern Democrat that voted against the legislation. I guess it's true: once a racist, always a racist. In 2009 Harry Reid compared Republicans opposing Obamacare to those who opposed civil rights in the 60s. Oops, Harry gets caught being ignorant, again, or was it another intentional lie? I guess I could be kind to the old gentleman and just claim that he is "historically challenged". At any rate, the truth remains intact: liberals did not then, nor do they now, have the best interests of the American women, minorities, and seasoned citizens at heart!

Even though the Republican Party is directly responsible for the passage of the Equal Rights Amendment in spite of liberal opposition, the liberals have told the lies long enough to have successfully rewritten that part of history. They are now allowed to claim they are the true champions of the little people; Republicans have a war on women, are racists, and wouldn't think twice about pushing grandma over the cliff in her wheelchair. The gullibility of half the American population is astonishing.

# GAY RIGHTS

*"It's about time we all faced up to the truth. If we accept the radical homosexual agenda, be it in the military or in marriage or in other areas of our lives, we are utterly destroying the concept of family."*     Alan Keyes

*"I oppose the attempts of homosexual activists to treat homosexual activity as a civil right to be protected and promoted by the government."*     Todd Akin

I am old enough to remember the days when the only meaning of the word "gay" was "happy". Let me jump right in and get started building on my "homophobe" title. I cannot understand why homosexuals are granted special rights and privileges based on their sexual preference. Heterosexuals have no special rights or privileges based on their sexual preference. What happened to that equal protection clause the liberals are always so eager to throw out? I long for the days when the homosexuals kept their private sex lives private, just as heterosexuals did. Gays begged everyone to stay out of their bedrooms and mind their own business. There were those who were exceptionally aggressive about "outing" what they considered to be an abhorrent lifestyle. I wish we could put that genie back in the bottle. What I mean by that is, *do not ever* take children to a gay pride parade. The sexual things that are done there are overlooked because of the homosexual purview, but would put a straight person in jail for public lewdness and probably several other city ordinances. What the gays wanted to keep private they now flaunt publicly.

Homosexuality flies in the face of the natural order of things. When God made man and woman he gave each a specific anatomy which were designed to work together. God gave all the animals of Earth similar anatomies and in Genesis told them "to go forth and multiply". I believe the God story. If you don't believe in God Almighty, but you worship Mother Nature, just keep in mind, regardless of who you give credit for producing man and woman and all the other creatures, the sexual process still works the same way: Tab A fits into Slot B. It works the same way in nearly all species on the planet. The male/female anatomy was specifically designed for procreation. There is no male on male or female on female orientation that serves that purpose. The only purpose for gay sex is recreational. Is there heterosexual recreational sex? Absolutely, but recreational sex was not the intended purpose of God's creation.

I find it amazing that 5% of the American population is gay, yet they control the other 95% of the population with the simple word "homophobe". It has an equally simple meeting: to be afraid of homosexuals. I'm not afraid of homosexuals; I just don't like the lifestyle. But I will not change my opinion based on being called names. With that in mind I am now labeled "homophobe" and "intolerant". I am absolutely tolerant of homosexuals and harbor no ill feelings toward the individual, just their sexual preference. The reason I'm called intolerant is because I refuse to kowtow to societal pressure to accept the homosexual lifestyle. The intolerant ones in this gay revolution are the gays themselves. They have enlisted a sufficient following of loud and obnoxious liberals to help advance their cause. What I find especially heinous is the fact that the liberal public school system is now "mainstreaming" the homosexual lifestyle to our children as early as kindergarten. Just another brainwashing technique used to advance a controversial liberal cause. That part of a child's upbringing should be left entirely up to the parents. As a nonbeliever in the cause I am treated like a leper or some other type of social misfit, to be publicly ostracized and ridiculed. Who is the intolerant one under those circumstances?

There have been cases brought by gays around the United States that should have been thrown out of court on first reading. One case was that of a professional photographer who respectfully refused to photograph a gay wedding based on her religious upbringing. The photographer was sued and found guilty of discrimination. Another case of gay intolerance was the treatment of an Arizona baker who refused to make a wedding cake for a gay wedding. He was found guilty of discrimination. I'm pretty sure there were plenty of other photographers and bakers the gay couples could have used to accomplish what they wanted. But their intolerance for nonbelievers reared its ugly head and resulted in forcing their gay lifestyle on normal Americans just trying to make a living. Christians had rights long before gays had rights but Christian beliefs are overridden by the bogus rights of gays. With the help of the liberal community and a handful of activist judges, these scenarios will become more and more prevalent throughout the United States.

The governor of Arizona, Jan Brewer, vetoed Arizona legislation called the "Religious Rights Bill". The purpose of the bill was to stop the targeting of Arizona businesses by the gay rights movement in order to advance their cause. I like Jan Brewer, but that move put her on my RINO list. She sold her soul to the devil because the National Football League was threatening to take away the 2015 Super Bowl from Arizona. The continued harassment and destruction of Arizona's business base will be far more detrimental to Arizona than the loss of a Super Bowl. The religious right is far more tolerant of gay rights than the gays are of religious rights! Homophobe is just a word like any other. If you know in your heart you don't hate homosexuals the word has no meaning to you. That works for all the liberal name-calling.

# ILLEGAL IMMIGRATION *and* AMNESTY

*"Amnesty is a terrible policy, and it's terrible politics. It's a terrible policy because you are rewarding people for breaking the law."*　　　　Tom Tancredo

*"Illegal aliens should not be granted amnesty and a path to citizenship. This would be a slap in the face to all those who have followed the law and come to America legally."*　　　　Jim Sensenbrenner

*"Amnesty is a big billboard, a flashing billboard, to the rest of the world that we don't really mean our immigration law."*　　　　Richard Lamm

No one can deny the importance of immigration to the history of the United States. Immigration has been said to be "the backbone of the American Society", and rightly so. But I am putting specific emphasis on it having been legal immigration. The diversity the legal immigration achieved is the cornerstone of the American population. The assimilation of so many different races and cultures is what has made this country great. The word immigration brings to my mind Ellis Island and the development of an American society that welcomed all comers. There is no moral comparison between those who come here legally and those who come here illegally beyond the pursuit for a better way of life. Legal immigrants came here wanting to be Americans and to be accepted in to this exceptional way of life. They gave up their country but were allowed to maintain most of their old country traditions and customs. They gave up their past citizenship and took an oath to defend America as their own.

I'm very passionate about this topic so prepare yourselves for a racist rant, not to be confused with a concerned, patriotic American rant. I won't spend a lot of time discussing legal immigration because I have no problem with that. I will spend a considerable amount of time discussing the current illegal invasion and the absolute ignorance of those supporting any form of illegal immigrant amnesty, which I perceive to be extremely detrimental to our American sovereignty. National origin does not create a special privilege when it comes to immigration. An immigrant is either legal or illegal. Stepping across the US border without permission and overstaying your welcome is illegal. The "wet foot/dry foot" policy allows Cuban nationals the privilege of staying in the United States if they can get a foot on US soil. If they're caught in the water they will be returned to Cuba. On the other hand, when Haitians land on US soil they still get deported.

It all sounds like it is based on some silly child's game. But it's no game to the Cubans and Haitians. If everyone that comes to America should receive equal status why are the Cubans and Haitians treated differently? Who gets called "racist" under these circumstances? I'm not expecting an answer to that question.

I am really wore out on the lack of distinction between legal and illegal immigration. When you put the word "illegal" in front of the word immigration it drastically changes the meaning. Illegal immigrants come here with no more in mind than to reap the benefits of American capitalism and American generosity. They have no desire to become Americans or be assimilated into American society even though that same American society gives everything to them. Then some have the audacity to wave their flags in protest marches because the generosity, in their eyes, is insufficient and we owe them more. They take jobs that Americans do want, now more than ever. They drive down the wage scale for all. There is no respect for the country that is hosting them even though that country protects them and cares for them. America does all this for them without asking for so much as a "thank you". America does all this for them even though the first thing they did was enter the United States illegally. Someone smarter than me can surely answer these questions: "If they are coming here seeking the means to have a better life, why can't they come here legally? Why do they have to be so ungrateful?"

So after all that bragging by the Obama administration that deportations drastically rose during his first five years in office turns out to be based on "doctored" numbers. The Center for Immigration Studies says all administrations prior to his counted deportations from inside the country as one number and all caught at the border as a separate number. Obama added them together to make it look like he was deporting more illegals than any president before him. Just another example of how he and his administration have no problem manipulating the truth. Now we find out that Obama is considering an executive order to stop deportations altogether. We have another example of a liberal claiming to do one thing but doing the exact opposite. At least this may stop him from lying about the number of people he is deporting.

Let's go a little deeper into the topic of deportation. The opponents of deportation are always quick to use the sad fact that deportation may deprive a family of one or both of its parents. Yet it is a fact here in the United States that prison terms deprive the family of one or both of its parents. Someone please explain to me what makes those two exact scenarios so

119

different. Another overly used argument comes in the form of how would we deport 12 million illegals? My answer to that is simple: self deportation. Self deportation would come in the form of what many would call "tough love". Immigration laws currently in effect prohibit employers from hiring illegals. Federal law prohibits the use of a social security number for any reason, including employment, if it were not specifically assigned to you by the Social Security Administration. Federal laws governing our very generous, taxpayer-funded, welfare system have been overlooked to allow illegal immigrants and their extended families to benefit from the system's programs. Several states even allow illegals to possess driver's licenses. If you prevent illegals from having American jobs, from having an illegal Social Security number, and end the illegal use of our welfare programs, you will generate instant self deportation. Turn out the lights, they all went home.

"Anchor babies" is another topic that sticks in my craw like peanut butter to the roof my mouth. The 14th Amendment to the U.S. Constitution is the basis for the "anchor baby" concept. Also known as the "equal protection" amendment, the 14th Amendment was adopted in July 1868 with the original intent to protect the citizenship rights of former slaves at the conclusion of the Civil War. The original intent was definitely the right thing to do but I don't believe the legislators realized what it would morph into in the 20th century. The term "anchor baby" first appeared around 1996 but didn't have much of a following until illegal immigrant amnesty was brought to the forefront during George Bush's presidency around 2006. If a baby is born on United States soil, regardless of the nationality of its parents, the baby can be considered a US citizen. The only other industrialized democracy on the planet that allows that type of citizenship is Canada. I cannot, under any circumstance, comprehend how such a ruling would in any way benefit American citizens. The only ones that benefit are the baby and the pregnant woman who, in the 11th hour before giving birth, made her way onto American soil and had her baby. The baby is now an American citizen and its parents are eligible to become American citizens in the future. But if liberals have their way, the baby's mother, father, and both of their extended families would have amnesty. Is America a great country or what?!

The US Department of Homeland security has estimated that there were 11 ½ million illegals in the United States as of the end of 2010. If all of these individuals were given amnesty and allowed to stay in the US the estimated costs of services necessary to sustain them over their lifetimes could run as high as $9 trillion. That is the net cost after factoring in $3 trillion of tax revenue obtained from the illegals. Services are all-inclusive: food, shelter, education, healthcare, etc., etc., etc.

Considering the fact that the bulk of illegal immigrants come from Mexico and they are the ones that will benefit from amnesty I'm going to cover a couple of items concerning their immigration laws. First of all, just the act of crossing into Mexico illegally is grounds for a prison sentence. If you get sick you better have cash to pay for medical care. Foreigners in Mexico can own land in the interior of the country but are severely limited to what they can own on the borders and the coastlines. There are no such restrictions for Mexicans in the US. A welfare system, as we know it, does not exist in Mexico. There is some food and medical assistance available to Mexicans but not to foreigners. Don't go there thinking you can access any of the scant services that are available to Mexican nationals. There are more American food stamps available to Mexicans then there are Mexican food stamps available to Mexicans. The United States Department of Agriculture advertises American food stamps in Mexico and encourages Mexicans to sign up for the benefits.

The reason any true conservative would support amnesty in any fashion completely eludes me. US immigration law requires anyone crossing into the US illegally be deported. It requires people overstaying a visa of any form be deported because they have become illegal by staying. It requires even legal immigrants who do bad things to other people be deported. We do not need to reform immigration law; we need to enforce the ones that are in effect currently. The sovereignty of the United States of America is on the verge of ultimate collapse under our current "open border" policies. There are many illegals crossing into the US that have good intentions; there are many illegals coming into the US from all over the world with very bad intentions. There is no way to distinguish between the two groups. All illegal immigration should be halted until we can find ways to make those distinctions.

It has always been my opinion that there is no way to curtail 100% of the illegal invasion but it could be held to a manageable level by a high-tech, high-rise fence. That would at least be a very good start to securing the border. In the areas where the US has fences in place the illegal entries are fewer than the areas of no fence. The illegals always manage to come up with countermeasures to defeat what the US does to keep them out, ranging from elaborate vehicle ramp systems to scale the fences to tunnels under the fences. But spending time trying to defeat US border fences and building tunnels slows them down and gives our US Border Patrol time to catch them in the act of trespass. Proponents of the illegal invasion say it is impossible to build a security fence on that length of border. Those in the current administration concur with that group. But coincidentally, this administration sent millions of taxpayer dollars and the United States Corps of Engineers to build that very type of security fence on the Israeli-Egyptian border. I guess the fence can be built across a desert. Wait, unless I flunked seventh grade geography, isn't the US southern border also a desert? I guess there must be some other reason we can't build the fence on our desert. President Reagan agreed to amnesty back in the 80s and the liberals agreed to build fence on the border. The liberals got the amnesty, Reagan got no fence. President Bush 2 made concessions to the liberals concerning illegals after the liberals agreed to build fence on the border. The liberals got their concessions, Bush got no fence. Is anyone besides me starting to notice a pattern here? In 2014 the liberals, with considerable Republican help, are again pursuing complete amnesty for illegals and everyone is concealing the fact that it is amnesty by calling it "immigration reform". Funny thing is, Republicans aren't bothering to negotiate for more fence because they know the liberals would never allow it to be built anyway.

The bottom line is, whether it's called amnesty or immigration reform, it will be devastating to the American economy. The claim that amnesty will involve only 12 million individuals is ridiculous and everyone that uses that number is a liar. Amnesty will allow those 12 million illegal individuals to remain and will allow them to bring into the United States their extended family members including children, parents, and siblings. If that number of extended family members would average five, $5 \times 12,000,000 = 60,000,000+$ the original 12 million equals 72 million. Seriously changes the statement that it would have very little effect on our economy, don't you think? The only number I made up is five, that number in reality will very likely be higher.

Let's do a little math for the Republican leaders and their followers who are in favor of amnesty. If half of the 72 million are voting age and 35% vote Republican then Republicans will have just short of 13 million new voters, yahoo! Now reality kicks in. Liberals get the other 65% which comes to over 23 million new voters. I'm not a big political campaign guru, but I've seen enough presidential elections to know that an additional 10 million votes for a liberal presidential candidate will make him a winner every time. I'm basing this on historical facts. Ronald Reagan received around 35% of the Latino vote in the 1984 presidential election. Ronald Reagan agreed to an amnesty just before he left office in the late 80s. George

H. W. Bush saw no bump in the percentage of Latino votes in the 1988 presidential election even though Reagan had done the amnesty on their behalf just months before. That is how I came up with the 35% I used in calculating the number of new voters for each party. Wake up Republicans, there's smoke in the air and the smoke is coming from your political ship as it burns and sinks under your feet. Republicans are trying their very best to be liked by the recipients of amnesty so they can stay in office. What they don't seem to understand is that they won't just be relegated to the status of permanent minority party, they will never receive enough votes to get in office. The newly anointed voters will vote for the liberal "Santa Claus" party no matter what the Republicans do.

There is a new "crisis" being used by the liberals to pressure and prod the Republicans into a quick but disastrous process of amnesty. The new crisis is the flood of Central American children across the US border with few accompanying adults. That is complete B. S.! Those children did not come up with that plan on their own. Adults devised the plan to put their own children in harm's way in order to force amnesty on the American people. That shows me how little they care about the children they claim to do everything for. The more I pay attention to and do research on the liberal/socialist methods of pursuing their ideology and agenda at all costs, the more I am disgusted. Obama said these "Dream Kids" are our future. He is exactly right. Let them all stay and take care of them and America's future will be changed forever.

# AFFIRMATIVE ACTION

*"Equal rights for all, special privileges for none."*　　　Thomas Jefferson

Affirmative Action was established by Executive Order 11246 issued by Lyndon Johnson in 1965. It was designed as a program to correct, and apologize for, past discrimination against minorities, women, and individuals with disabilities. Even though the intentions were good, results of the program have been less than stellar. As with all liberal programs regardless of its original intention, it has come to be purely a vote-buying scheme. The implication of the entire program asserts that none of the above listed individuals can do anything for themselves nor better themselves without government intervention. Most women, minorities, and people with disabilities are offended by that implication and they have every right to be. I have never understood the thought process that allows discrimination against one set of individuals to prevent discrimination against another set of individuals. Remember the old saying: "two wrongs don't make a right". Affirmative Action is a circular motion that continually bites everyone in the circle on the posterior.

America has survived and thrived for 225 years by honoring and rewarding the smartest and the best in every aspect of American life. If you are sick you want the best doctor available. If you are going to be assigned to a Navy vessel you want the best welder to build your ship. When you send your precious children off to school you want the best bus driver at the wheel and the best teachers at the school when the kids arrive. Affirmative Action may prevent those scenarios from being fulfilled. Affirmative Action eliminates the advancement of the best and the brightest and rewards mediocrity.

Lopsided college entrance applications reward students of lesser abilities an advantage in acceptance to the college. Their race or sex will get them into college quicker than their high school grades will. An Hispanic girl in a wheelchair with a C+ average has a better chance getting into college than a white male with straight As. Is that a racist and sexist comment or just sour grapes? Call it what you will, it is a fact of American higher education brought on by the enforcement of Affirmative Action. An unintended consequence or at least a result of the Affirmative Action in college is what happened to college sports under a policy affectionately known as Title IX. Title IX made it illegal for colleges to discriminate against women in their sports programs. In other words, even though there may be only six girls that wanted a female lacrosse team, the college had to find money in their sports budget to fund a female lacrosse team. If sports funds were limited, as is the case in many small colleges, currently funded boys sports programs may have to be eliminated. A male sport could not be funded if the mirror female sport could not be funded. The male sport has to end.

Hiring quotas required employers to give an advantage to minorities and women when considering hiring a new employee. The employer is not necessarily allowed to select the most qualified applicant; he must take into consideration the number of minorities and women already in his employ. If he's not at the minimum required federal quotas, he is limited to who he can hire. I am not saying minorities and women are inferior in skills, abilities, or intelligence only that they have an advantage.

My point to all of this is: for all the screaming and tantrums the liberals employ in an effort to "level the playing field", in the end, Affirmative Action definitely tilts the field. "Affirmative Action prevents discrimination" is a classic example of an oxymoron. "Affirmative Action" is discrimination. There is no such thing as "reverse discrimination". Discrimination is discrimination regardless of who is on the receiving end.

I will express one last racist thought on this topic and then go on to a different chapter. Why are professional sports exempt from quotas or any form of affirmative action in the player rosters of their teams? Don't give me the argument that minority athletes are better overall athletes than whites. Whether that's true or not it shouldn't give sports teams a pass on leveling the playing field. (a twofer pun; am I good or what?) NFL teams were instructed by the NFL commission to make all efforts and exhaust all possibilities in hiring black coaches before settling for a white coach. There is no such directive given when hiring players. I'm not complaining mind you, I just felt the need to remind my readers that political correctness has no place in this book.

# POVERTY, WELFARE *and* ENTITLEMENTS

*"Welfare's purpose should be to eliminate, as far as possible, the need for its own existence."*                                                                            Ronald Reagan

*"The democracy will cease to exist when you take away from those who are willing to work and give to those who would not."*                        Thomas Jefferson

*"I predict future happiness for Americans if they can prevent the government from wasting the labors of the people under the pretense of taking care of them."*                                                                                        Thomas Jefferson

Sorry Gentlemen: we failed.

Americans for the most part, have not experienced true poverty since the 1960s. If you doubt that statement look at the pictures on the TV ads by various "feed the children" organizations. You can't duplicate those scenes anywhere in America. Americans do not live with open sewage ditches nor do we drink brown water from a local river. Many families, in countries too numerous to mention, live on pennies a day. They could live on the dropped and discarded change they could find on a 7-11 parking lot. The establishment of the "welfare state" in the 1960s has made current claims of American poverty an urban myth. The current 2014 Health and Human Services (HHS) poverty guidelines are set at $29,812 for a family of four. That number reflects the amount of personal income of that family but does not include any taxpayer funding spent on behalf of that same family. In 2011 the taxpayers provided an average of $60,000 per poverty level household through 80 federal poverty programs. It would be cheaper to just identify those poverty households and write them a check for $60,000. The reason that can't happen is that a large portion of the $60,000 spent pays the operation, administration, and wages of the federal bureaucrats who run those 80 agencies. Those numbers provide a little insight into the wasteful spending of taxpayer funds. How, and more importantly, why does it take 80 separate agencies to administer help to poverty level families? If all the money ends up in the same place don't you think that 79 of those agencies are redundant?

In the 1960s when the welfare state was born, 16% of American households were at poverty level. Fifty years and several trillion dollars later, 16% of American households are still at poverty level. Since the programs we have now don't seem to be working maybe we need to try something different. The things that continue to keep poverty alive are the

126

actual welfare system policies themselves. If you are supported by $60,000 worth of taxpayer funds without having to get off the couch why would you want to go to work each day to make $30,000? Not much incentive there, right? Poverty breeds poverty, literally. If you receive additional funds from several different agencies for each child you bring into the world that's money in the bank and food on the table. That is an incentive. It is typical liberal backward reasoning that keeps the neediest among us dependent on the federal government for their most basic needs. Our welfare system is the direct cause of the loss of the two parent family which in turn has resulted in the loss of parental control of our most precious commodity: our children. With no discipline they are allowed to be disruptive in the classroom guaranteeing themselves a worthless education; behave badly on the streets; and eventually end up as wards of the state prison system. All of that thanks to our "cradle-to-grave" welfare system. It just makes a person proud all over to be so helpful.

*"The family has always been the cornerstone of American society. Our families nurture, preserve, and pass on to each succeeding generation the values we share and cherish, values that are the foundation of our freedoms."* Ronald Reagan

# FOREIGN POLICY *and* AID

*"Peace, commerce and honest friendship with all nations; entangling alliances with none."*
                                                                    Thomas Jefferson

*"We are for aiding our allies by sharing some of our material blessings with those nations which share in our fundamental beliefs, but we are against doling out money government to government, creating bureaucracy, if not socialism, all over the world. We set out to help 19 countries. We are helping 107. We spent $146 billion. With all that money, we bought a $2 million yacht for Haile Selassie (Emperor of Ethiopia circa 1930 to 1974). We bought dress suits for Greek undertakers, extra wives for Kenyan government officials. We bought a 1,000 TV sets for a place where they have no electricity."*   Ronald Reagan

US taxpayer dollars are spent around the world on many worthy causes. But US taxpayers also send a lot of money to dictators, outlaw countries, and worthless causes. We send money to these world "leaders" who systematically steal the money for personal gain. Their people continue to live in squalor and starve. I can't justify that level of ignorance on the part of our elected leaders. Many American foreign policies, including aid, are completely out of sync with the American population. Many Americans, including myself, feel we taxpayers expend far too much blood and treasure overseas. That is not an isolationist attitude because we also know the necessity of maintaining a US presence around the world. That US presence must be in the form of both financial and military. But there are, and will continue to be, many foreign situations that we need to keep our collective noses out of. There are so many situations that are not our concern. We inject our opinions in places where they are not welcome. Worse yet, we inject our presence in places where we are not welcome. Simply put, we need to mind our own business.

We spend a lot of money trying to buy foreign friends. You can't make someone like you by giving them something. It doesn't matter what that something is: it can be cash; it can be food and/or farm aid; it can be medical aid; it can be technology, business or military; or all of the above; it still won't make them like you! Most people hate charity but will accept it and turn around and bite the hand that provides the generosity. I am tired of hearing the disrespect and hatred of the United States that echoes from around the world. There is no country on the face of the earth that is more generous to all than the United States of America.

We need to curtail military involvement around the world. We need to stop being the world's policeman for petty tyrants that abuse their people. We can't be everything to everyone. Our financial generosity must have a limit. We need to spend more American dollars on Americans. We have a national debt which will wreak havoc on the American economy far into the foreseeable future. The American taxpayers and their heirs and descendents will be paying that debt for a very long time.

The current US Administration seems to have trouble distinguishing between America's allies and America's enemies. The Administration does not hesitate to send taxpayer dollars and military supplies to the Muslim Brotherhood in Egypt, to Hamas, the Palestinian Authority, and several other terrorist organizations and countries that long for the destruction of both Israel and the United States of America. The current US Administration has supported the overthrow of dictators in Libya, Egypt, and Syria with no consideration of how poorly the "newly-in-charge" will govern. So far, in the cases of Libya and Egypt, the results have been chaotic and deadly.

With all due respect to our State Department, their foreign-policy advisers, and our current guilt-ridden, apologetic Administration, we do not owe the world anything. If we had adults in charge they would cut off foreign aid and close US embassies in offending countries! If that drives those countries to pursue aid from one of our enemies, so be it. Let our enemies expend their blood and treasure for a while. I wonder how long it would take before we see them back at our doorstep, hat in hand, asking for help, with every intention of biting our hand again when we extend it; after they receive their treat of course. And we will extend it again because that's how Americans are: naïve and generous to a fault.

I'm going to add a few comments about the United Nations rather than do a separate chapter. The United States provides a disproportionate amount of the funding and all of the housing of the global dictators and thugs "good ole boys club". The United Nations is the largest group of ungrateful, whining miscreants and criminals ever assembled in one place on the planet. They disregard our laws, overstay their welcome, and abuse our generosity. With their infamous "diplomatic immunity", they have carte blanche to run roughshod on American soil. They can't be held accountable for so much as a parking ticket. They have more privileges on American soil than Americans have. The revenues generated by the presence of the UN entourage would easily be offset by the revenues generated in the absence of the UN entourage. The UN buildings and/or the property they set on would be easily absorbed back into their financially-based surroundings.

The sudden availability of high dollar apartments could have the beneficial effect of lower rentals in the area. I always smile when I see UN stories on TV because I think of Rush Limbaugh's depiction of the UN General Assembly as the bar scene from Star Wars.

# INTERNAL REVENUE SERVICE *and* TAXES

*"Our federal tax system is, in short, utterly impossible, utterly unjust and completely counterproductive. It reeks with injustice, and is fundamentally un-American."* Ronald Reagan

*"The problem is not that people are taxed too little, the problem is that government spends too much."* Ronald Reagan

According to the Tax Foundation taxpayers will have paid their tax debt to government for calendar year 2014 on April 21. That is 111 days of you working for the government. The government gets 30% of your paychecks. American taxpayers will pay the federal government $3 trillion and state governments $1.5 trillion. That is more than all Americans pay each year for food, clothing, and housing combined. In other words, American taxpayers give up more money to maintain our government tax systems than they do to maintain their own necessities of life. What is wrong with that picture?

Regardless of a long history of federal government abuses, many Americans continue to believe government policies and laws enforced by gun toting, SWAT style officials is okay in America. I'm here to tell you it is not. When law enforcement agents knock down your door with guns in hand to look at your tax records, there's something wrong with the American system of law enforcement. The old adage of "innocent until proven guilty" no longer applies in America. In fact, it has been completely turned around. Most law enforcement agencies from local all the way up to federal treat you as guilty and you are required to prove your innocence. The IRS is one of the leading agencies that promotes that way of thinking. If they feel you may be hiding a dime from them, they can make the next several years of your life a living hell. The mere mention of the IRS sends chills down the spines of most Americans and for good reason. Since its inception the IRS has been the most feared and despised of the federal enforcement agencies. Most enforcement agencies can fine you and/or jail you. The IRS can fine you, jail you and take all of you and your family's worldly possessions for the rest of your lives. An IRS audit is never a pleasant experience. To make matters worse the IRS has been used by several administrations to harass, bully, intimidate, silence, and bankrupt political opponents.

Obama's administration is no exception and is the latest to use the IRS to silence and harass his political opponents. The use of the IRS to prevent Conservative political groups from operating by delaying or denying their nonprofit status is at the very least immoral and at its worst is criminal. Lois Lerner, who was the IRS agency head during the time that the conservative applications were being denied, has pled "The Fifth" to prevent incriminating herself during questioning by the House of Representatives investigation of the scandal. The bulk of the discrimination against the conservative political groups just happens to coincide with the two years prior to the 2012 presidential election. There is no link between the IRS and Mr. Obama concerning the scandal, yet. But I have no fear in saying that the liberals at all levels of the IRS would do this as a favor to Mr. Obama knowing there would be no repercussions from him or Attorney General Eric Holder and his Justice Department. There are however documented statements by three high ranking liberal congressman, Senators Chuck Schumer and Carl Levine and House Representative Elijah Cummings, encouraging the IRS to investigate and even prosecute some of the conservative groups in question. There is definitely a serious problem when a government can punish American citizens for their political views. In 2014 the IRS is giving out $62 million of taxpayer dollars in bonuses. I guess the big dogs at the IRS are getting their treats for doing Obama's dirty deeds and successfully leaving his name out of the scandal.

The IRS scandals never seem to end. Just a couple years ago the IRS made national news for their complete lack of fiscal responsibility. They spent millions and millions of taxpayer dollars on themselves with no regards to the plight of the American people they take the money from. They treat themselves to fancy hotels, expensive food, champagne, and hot tubs all at taxpayer expense. They have ridiculous skits and plays that require expensive costumes and sets to produce, and when caught, feel no remorse and actually defend their waste of taxpayer funds. One would have to assume that they feel entitled to the use of the money since they are the ones that are collecting it in the first place. All they have to do to make up the difference is perform more audits, charge more penalties and interest, and find a few new ways to milk the taxpayers for more of their hard-earned cash.

The really scary part about all of this is the fact that this corrupt and dysfunctional agency has been put in charge of collecting unpaid premiums due the federal government because of Obamacare. I'm going to tell you why the IRS was put in charge of these collections rather than a new federal insurance agency. Everyone is already afraid of the IRS so will be reluctant to not comply. Another reason is because the IRS already has the means to make the collection easy. Beginning with your 2014 tax year you will have to prove to the IRS that you have an insurance policy that meets the minimum guidelines set by Obamacare. If the insurance you have does not meet the guidelines or you have no insurance at all, you will be charged a penalty. If you owe a penalty and fail to include that in your 2014 taxes due on April 15, 2015 the IRS has the authority to keep your tax refund. If you have a refund coming but it is insufficient to cover the penalty you will receive a bill from the IRS for the balance due. If you have no refund coming you better hope you received enough taxpayer assistance to have purchased the insurance in the first place. If you're confused with what Obama care has done to this point, just wait and see what happens when it is fully implemented. It will anger you as much as it confuses you. No one, including Nancy Pelosi, knew how prophetic her words would be: "We won't know what's in the Affordable Care Act until we pass it".

It would surprise me if there's a single person in the United States that doesn't feel the federal tax codes need amended, shortened, or outright repealed. I'm in favor of the latter. No one including the IRS can comprehend the tangle of regulations put on the US taxpayer. You could put IRS employees and high dollar tax attorneys together in the same room and they still wouldn't be able to answer your tax questions in a unified voice. I know people who work in an accounting office. The office deals with all forms related to the IRS. They said they have called different people at various IRS offices around the country for answers to specific questions and guidance in the proper methods of completing the volumes of forms and reports. IRS agents at different offices, and some agents in the same office, will give different answers to the same specific question. Many times they just don't have an answer at all. If they don't know, how in the world are we supposed to know? Rather than address the problems that exist in the incomprehensible current tax codes in an effort to simplify them, the IRS and the Federal bureaucrats continually add more confusion to the code with additional codes. The amendments and revisions for the tax year 2012 left a total of 73,608 pages in the code. No wonder no one knows what's in it.

IRS tax codes only need consist of one paragraph and here it is: "Each individual that had income during the previous tax year will be considered an individual taxpayer. There is no longer a joint income filing status. There will be no deductions allowed of any sort. There will be no deductions for dependents including children. You should be taking care of your elderly parents as restitution for the many years they cared for you. If you elect to have children, pay for them. If your gross income is $20,000 or less, send in 3% of your income. If your income is between

$20,001 and $50,000, send in 5% of your income. If your income is over $50,001, send in 10% of your income. There will be no deductions, no loopholes, and no amendments to the gross income. If you have a business your taxable income will be determined in the following manner: You will be allowed to deduct the rental cost or the mortgage payment and interest on your place of business. You will be allowed to deduct utilities costs for that same place of business. If you have vehicles or equipment necessary to the operation of the business you may deduct the annual costs of same. You may deduct costs of employees limited to wages or salaries, insurance, and applicable funds going directly to an employee pension plan. Unlike at the IRS, company picnics and getaways and the amenities pertaining to such including, but not limited to, room, board, extracurricular activities, and booze, will not be deductible. There will be no tax loopholes, no hiding revenue in offshore accounts, no non-taxable financial shelters or trust accounts, and don't bother to hide cash under your mattress; we have ways of finding it. After your few deductions are allowed, please send in the appropriate percentage of the net amount of income as listed in the above individual income categories. If you do not comply to the fullest, your place of business will be raided by a heavily armed SWAT team headed up by Lois Lerner". See how simple that would be. It took less than 300 words to write new tax codes. That breakdown of taxes, if enforced as written, would net the federal government 10 times the revenue they currently confiscate from the American taxpayers.

I got audited by the IRS in 1970 or '71 when I filed an amended return because I failed to disclose a $150 college scholarship when I submitted my original return. To my recollection, that is my only encounter with the IRS beyond sending in annual returns. I feel safe in saying: that audit will probably not remain an isolated incident once this book hits the shelves. "On the advice of counsel I invoke my Fifth Amendment rights and respectfully refuse to answer on the grounds that I might incriminate myself." "On the advice of counsel I invoke my Fifth Amendment rights and respectfully refuse to answer on the grounds that I might incriminate myself." "On the advice of counsel I invoke my Fifth Amendment rights and respectfully refuse to answer on the grounds that I might incriminate myself." If I practice diligently enough and maintain a good poker face I should be safe, right Lois?

# SOCIAL SECURITY

*"Back in 1935, there were 42 workers for every retiree. Today, in regards to Social Security, we only have three workers for every retiree."* Dennis Hastert

*"More young people believe they'll see a UFO than that they'll see their own Social Security benefits."* Mitch McConnell

*"We shall make the most lasting progress if we recognize that Social Security can furnish only a base upon which each one of our citizens may build his individual security through his own individual efforts."* Franklin D. Roosevelt

Even FDR, the president that established Social Security, admits that it was not intended to be a full retirement plan. I am guessing he did not realize that merely 80 years in the future it would amount to a $12 trillion unfunded mandate.

I will disclose that I am on Social Security. I started it at 62 as a result of some medical issues. I am not on Social Security disability. There is only enough money in my social security account for me to draw on for about three more years. After that I am using someone else's money. My kids, your kids, my grandkids, your grandkids and maybe even you will be paying for me. That doesn't leave anything in your account for your retirement. On the other hand, if this book is successful, I'll get off Social Security and leave your money alone. Tell your friends to buy the book.

According to the Social Security Administration Press Office "Basic Facts", as of April 2, 2014 there are around 58 million Americans receiving $863 billion in social security benefits annually: 38 million retired workers; 3 million dependents of retired workers; 9 million disabled workers; 2 million dependents of disabled workers; 6 million on survivor benefits.

The "Social Security Lockbox" is a myth. All the trillions of taxpayer and employer dollars sent in to Social Security over the 79 years since FDR initiated it have been spent by the federal government to buy votes. The piles of Social Security funds were too tempting for the federal government to ignore. The funds have been used over the years for the gluttonous social programs such as welfare, Medicare, Medicaid, and every other vote buying program the feds could conceive. Who votes for a politician that doesn't give them free stuff? That free stuff has been paid for with your Social Security money. Open the Social Security lockbox and you'll find nothing but dust, cobwebs, and a very large stack of IOUs. The people in possession of the keys to the lockbox turned out to be very untrustworthy. Is it not theft or at least fraud if you spend someone else's money without their permission? Private citizens are prosecuted and jailed regularly for Ponzi schemes. Social Security is the granddaddy of Ponzi schemes and it has been played on the American people by their elected leaders since 1935.

The following information was obtained from the US Social Security website. Social Security was originally designed to kick in at the retirement age of 65. In 1940, when monthly benefits began to be paid, men who reached the age of 65 could expect to receive Social Security benefits for 12.7 years. The problem for the American male population in 1940 was less than 54% of them reached the age of 65. Also, there were only 9 million Americans at or over 65 in 1940. The designers did not factor in the increase in life expectancy years or the enormous number of baby boomers after World War II who are now at retirement age. Currently, men reaching the age of 65 can expect to draw Social Security for 19 years. Approximately 77% of the American population will reach age 65. According to the 2010 census there were 40,267,984 people in America 65 years or older. All liberal social programs fail to consider the unintended consequences. A person living for 19 additional years was not factored in when devising their Ponzi scheme. Even after realizing the error of their ways, they have continued to spend the money in advance. The program was doomed to fail for lack of funds. But the Washington bureaucrats rode in on their white horses, once again, to save us lowly taxpayers from their ignorance. The solution, in their eyes, was simple: raise the amount of Social Security funds taxpayers have to pay into the system; raise the mandatory retirement age to 67. The Social Security system is still broke and is still doomed to fail requiring even more drastic measures be taken in an attempt to save the program. Do not be surprised in the near future when the mandatory retirement age will be 70. It warms my heart to know that our elected officials take such good care of us taxpayers. It warms their hearts knowing they take even better care of themselves.

The lawmakers have what is called the Federal Employee Retirement System. They can retire at age 62 if they have as little as 5 years of taxpayer funded salaries. They can retire at age 50 if they have 20 years of taxpayer funded salaries. They can retire at any age with 25 years of taxpayer funded salaries. The bulk of this information comes from the Congressional Research Service "Retirement Benefits for Members of Congress" dated March 19, 2014. At the start of the 2013 federal fiscal year, there were 527 retired Congress members drawing some form of pension from the

American taxpayers. Of those, 312 were receiving an annual pension in excess of $71,000. If they retire at age 50 they can expect to feed at the taxpayer trough for 34 years to the age of 84. I will not thank you on their behalf, but they should.

Federal employees did not pay into Social Security until 1984. Prior to that they participated in a government pension plan that they did not have to contribute to; paid for entirely by taxpayers. They now pay into Social Security the same 6.2% that we do. Now when they retire they will receive a federal pension and a Social Security pension. Currently a congressman receives $174,000 base salary; plus additional money paid to them as committee members, and additional money paid to them if they are committee chairman. All three of these conditions can add up to over $200,000 per year. The pension funds they receive are based on their highest three years of salaries. Private sector Social Security benefits are based on the average of 35 years of salaries. If you didn't work a total of 35 years, each year of non-contribution is assigned a zero which lowers the average considerably; another method our elected officials saw fit to use to prevent the return of your money. By the way, if you want copies of your Social Security payment records the Social Security Administration will send you a copy of each year for $15. If you are into discount specials and would like a copy of 40 years of your social security payment history it will cost you $80.

I would like to thank all of you taxpayers who will be paying into the Social Security system after June 2017 when my lockbox funds are depleted. My monthly check will be dependent upon you paying in your required 6.2%. The federal government will place an IOU with my name on it in the lockbox in your behalf.

Here's a thought: When a person retires he/she should have the option of taking their pension in monthly installments or in one lump sum just like you can if you win the lotto, but without them keeping 60% of your money.

# UNITED STATES COURT SYSTEM

*"A free people claim their rights as derived from the laws of nature, and not as the gift of their magistrate."*                                                    Thomas Jefferson

*"One single object will merit the endless gratitude of the society, that of restraining the judges from usurping legislation."*                            Thomas Jefferson

*"On every question of the Constitution let us carry ourselves back to the time when the Constitution was adopted; recollect the spirit manifested in the debates instead of trying what meaning may be squeezed out of the text, or invented against it; conform to the probable one in which it was passed."*
                                                                           Thomas Jefferson

No one wants to talk about the fragile nature of the makeup of the United States Supreme Court. Republicans don't need to talk about it because for the last several years it has a high percentage of making the right decisions in the protection the U.S. Constitution. The liberals don't want to talk about it because they don't want to prematurely bring attention to the changes that will take place in the membership of the court in the next few years. Stephen Breyer is 76, Anthony Kennedy and Antonin Scalia are both 78, and Ruth Bader Ginsburg is 81. Replacing Breyer or Ginsburg will not change anything. Obama will completely reverse the ideological makeup of the sitting court by replacing either Kennedy or Scalia before he leaves office. His appointments of hard-core leftist judges Elena Kagan and Sonia Sotomayor in addition to judges Breyer and Ginsburg gives Obama four solidly dependable liberal votes on the bench. The liberals have their fingers crossed that one of the right-leaning judges will be gone from the court during Obama's tenure. It wouldn't have to happen that quickly except with all the administration scandals including Benghazi, there is no guarantee that Hillary will be in place to affect the changes. Judges Samuel Alito, Clarence Thomas, and Scalia are solid defenders of the U.S. Constitution. Chief Justice John Roberts and Justice Kennedy are typically defenders of the Constitution although Roberts is a little shaky when he gets called names by the liberals, as witnessed by the contortions he put himself and the court through over the Obamacare decision.

The court has been for the last several years the only thing between the United States being a Republic or a tyranny. Representative governmental politics should not be confused with a democracy. As witnessed by the treatment of the vast Christian population in America by the government on behalf of the gay community: the majority does not rule. The few can control the many with the backing of the court system. Liberal ideology cannot win in a voting booth. The only chance that liberalism/socialism has to maintain any semblance of power is to control the courts. That is why it is so critical to the liberals to overload the courts in their favor. Having five liberal/socialist judges on the US Supreme Court will guarantee that liberal ideology trumps the U.S. Constitution. Appointing young, idealistic, and inexperienced liberal/socialists like Kagan and Sotomayor to the US Supreme Court will guarantee liberals favorable outcomes for many years to come.

We have seen so many times when citizens of a state have passed laws with overwhelming results only to have them overturned by a liberal federal judge. The only recourse the non-liberals have is to appeal to the US Supreme Court for relief from the progressive ideology. The liberal Ninth Circuit Court is the most overturned court in the nation. That alone tells you that the hard-core liberal ideology is not defendable. Republicans take for granted that all members of the US Supreme Court are nonpartisan and beyond reproach. They hope the justices will base their decisions on the United States Constitution without bias or favoritism. Liberals on the other hand have no such naïveté. They know that they must control the court system in order to advance their socialist agenda. Republican presidents have nominated people to the US Supreme Court that were not conservative with the hopes that they would be unbiased and unflappable and that's where the naïveté comes in. No past liberal president has ever nominated a conservative to the Supreme Court, and it will never happen in the future. George Bush nominated one Latino man, one woman, and one white guy to the US Supreme Court, both men, Alito and Roberts were confirmed. The woman, Harriet Miers, was opposed by the Republicans for a couple reasons: many thought she was not qualified for the position or may allow some of her social ideologies to affect her interpretation of the Constitution. It was said Bush nominated her simply because of her sense of loyalty to him. Regardless of his reason for nominating her in the first place, with such Republican opposition, Mr. Bush promptly threw her under the bus. He walked away without ever defending her which left her no choice but to ask Bush to withdraw her nomination. I was pretty upset at him over that.

By the way, the liberals who claim the moral high ground in defense of blacks continually prove they only defend liberal blacks. Does anyone recall the vicious and disgusting treatment that Clarence Thomas received from the Democrats during his congressional review for a position on the US Supreme Court in 1991?

Thomas Jefferson was an adamant supporter of properly applied justice within our American court system. He seemed to have a caveat that appeared in much of his writing: he was completely opposed to judicial activism. He did not believe the U.S. Constitution was what we now call a "living document" to be interpreted and revised at a whim. This quote by Thomas Jefferson makes my point: "Laws are made for man of ordinary understanding and should, therefore, be construed by the ordinary rules of common sense. Their meaning is not to be sought for in metaphysical subtleties which may make anything mean everything or nothing at pleasure." Jefferson did not say that there could never be changes to the Constitution but that we should make every effort to interpret it as written.

# BANKING

*"I sincerely believe that banking establishments are more dangerous than standing armies, and that the principal of spending money to be paid by posterity, under the name of funding is but swindling futurity on a large scale."*
                                                              Thomas Jefferson

Let's start with the Troubled Asset Relief Program (TARP) that George Bush initiated. In the context of this chapter we will also clear up a couple liberal attempts to rewrite history. In 2008 TARP allowed the Department of the Treasury to spend $700 billion of taxpayer funds to purchase or guarantee questionable mortgages of several lending institutions. The ironic thing is the federal government created the bad mortgages (subprime) with the Community Reinvestment Act of 1977. CRA was forced on the American banking institutions by liberals in the Carter administration. The act required lending institutions to loan money to questionable borrowers to buy homes. In many cases, the banks were not even allowed to ask about, much less confirm, income status of the borrower. You can't get any dumber than liberal policy! The banks knew many of the loans would not be repaid.

In the early years of George Bush's administration he begged Congress to get control of the CRA because it was very, very bad legislation. George Bush warned everyone the housing market was in serious trouble. Liberals, in so many words, called him Chicken Little for claiming "the sky was falling". Lo and behold, in 2007 the sky fell, or more accurately the housing bubble burst. Fannie Mae and Freddie Mac (both home mortgage holders affiliated with the federal government), J.P. Morgan Chase, AIG, Wells Fargo, and many other large financial institutions were stuck with subprime mortgages that were not worth the paper they were written on. I could have used those mortgage papers the five years I used an outhouse growing up. But I digress.

So there we were in 2008 after 30 years of writing garbage mortgages at the behest of the liberals in the federal government. That same federal government that screwed up in the first place now decides to use taxpayer funds to clean up their mess. No surprise there, it's always been done that way in Washington. The federal government decided that the banks holding the worthless mortgages were "too big to fail" and must be saved. If the federal government does not bail them out with taxpayer money the world economy will collapse and everyone will be standing in food lines. No company is too big to fail. It's called "capitalistic extinction".

So what happens is the big banks not only were saved but thrived using the taxpayer money. Whew, close call. Many had extra money to buy out smaller existing banks or open new affiliate banks or even buy foreign banks with American taxpayer funds. Great gig when you can get it. Meanwhile, the taxpayers that funded the bailouts for the rich guys are living in houses that were purchased at the peak of the housing market just before the collapse. My wife and I fall in that category of mortgage holders. Our mortgage has changed hands five times in eight years. We are paying for a house that is worth 25% of what we paid for it. We will never have equity in our home. Neither of us will live long enough to see its value returned. By the way, even with $700 billion spent by the United States, much of the world economic market still collapsed: e.g. Greece, Spain, etc.

Liberals are attempting to revise history by saying because the housing bubble burst during George Bush's administration that makes him responsible. They don't remember him standing up and telling them it was about to happen and they should do something about it immediately. They conveniently forgot that the liberal backed CRA of 1977 was what started the housing market on the road to its ultimate catastrophic collapse. Their liberal policies of the previous 30 years had nothing to do with it?

Another clarification and a fact Mr. Obama and the liberals would rather you didn't know: George Bush only spent half of the $700 billion. After the November 2008 election President-elect Obama asked George Bush to request the release of the balance of the money so that it would be available to him immediately upon his assuming the presidency. Mr. Bush did as requested. But Obama wanted more taxpayer money. In February 2009 he requested an additional $787 billion "to save and create jobs". What he got was the American Recovery and Reinvestment Act of 2009 with a blank check in the amount of $831 billion. So now he has $350 billion left over from Bush's TARP money and an additional $831 billion added to his discretionary slush fund. You now know where he gets the taxpayer money that he wastes on his campaign donor's "green" projects. Also, liberals claim the stimulus increased employment somewhere between 1.5 million and 3.5 million jobs. With 12 million Americans unemployed I'm a little skeptical of their numbers. But let's assume their numbers are correct and do a little math: if you spent $831 billion "to save and create" 3.5 million jobs that computes to having spent $2,374,285 per job. Ladies and gentlemen as comedian Ron White says: "You can't fix stupid".

Obama made the determination on his own that the United Autoworkers union was "too big to fail". Obama sent $80 billion of the original taxpayer TARP funds to General Motors and Chrysler who were holding the bag on billions in car loans and union pension accounts. That use of funds was one of Obama's original union vote buying schemes. General Motors used American taxpayer TARP money in China to double their production of exports from their Chinese plants. It's a good thing they used TARP money first to appease the American GM autoworkers union by stabilizing their ailing retirement programs; having done that the 130,000 vehicles they made in China wasn't as big a slap in the face to the American autoworkers. I'm not an auto worker but it makes me want to be a Ford man. By the way, Mr. Obama has claimed that GM has paid back all the TARP funds, they have not and probably never will. Taxpayers lose again.

You've heard the saying "insanity is doing something over and over again but expecting a different result". Ladies and gentlemen, we are presently, in 2014, about to witness a level of insanity that is mind-boggling. A mere six years after America experienced one of the worst economic downturns in history as a result of the collapse of the housing market, Mr. Obama has said that in order to revive that collapsed housing market we must again require banks to issue subprime mortgages using the same methods of lending that got us in the housing situation in the first place. Liberal/socialist ideology just keeps on giving and giving; or more accurately it keeps on taking and taking.

You can't ignore the obvious "elephant in the room". A precedent has been set that the banking industry and very large corporations have undoubtedly taken notice of: regardless of the financial holes the government puts them in or they dig for themselves in the future, they now know they are deemed by the federal government too big to fail. That same government will save them with taxpayer cash that they may or may not have to pay back. You can just imagine the unencumbered risk-taking and financial shenanigans that will go on when the taxpayers are covering their financial bad behavior.

Federal bureaucrats continue to legislate economic issues based on bogus Keynesian Economic Theory: the most effective way to revive a stagnant economy (when taxpaying consumers are not spending their cash) is for the federal government to spend the taxpayer's money in their behalf; "if the taxpayers refuse to spend their money we will spend it for them". The classic "Catch 22": when the economy is bad people are smart enough to save their discretionary money in case the economy gets worse; which slows the economy down; which in turn makes the government feel the need to boost the economy by taking the money away from the taxpayers that have saved it and spend it in their behalf. This is a "Catch 22" and a "vicious circle" all rolled into one.

Let's talk a little about the Federal Reserve ("The Fed"). Most Americans think The Fed is a branch of the Washington bureaucracy. It is not. The Federal Reserve is actually a group of private bankers that answer to no higher power, including our federal government. This group of bankers is allowed to set interest rates and the value of our currency, which in turn has a considerable amount of control over every aspect of our economy. The member banks determine which financial institutions will receive bailout money. Several of the banks that received bailout money are Federal Reserve members. Can you say "conflict of interest"? The president does have control of the money that the banks get and also is allowed to choose the Federal Reserve Chairman. The Fed prints money as they see fit or at the request of the administration then loans it to the government. The administration can in turn take that play money and use it for whatever purpose they deem necessary. A president's influence on the economy is based on the borrowed money he spends and how he spends it, which still makes him the ultimate villain if he spends it improperly or a hero if he spends it correctly. Americans have long believed that when something happened that affected or changed the economy, good or bad, it was a result of that administration's policies. That is mostly true. The president can spend all the money he wants as long as the Fed agrees to print it for him. It is bad enough that there is an organization that has that much control but it is made worse by the fact that it's controlled by individuals that can't be held accountable by our voting process. Pretty scary stuff can be found with a minor amount of research!

*"I believe that banking institutions are more dangerous to our liberties than standing armies. If the American people ever allow private banks to control the issue of their currency, first by inflation, then by deflation, the banks and corporations that will grow up around (the banks) will deprive the people of all property until their children wake-up homeless on the continent their fathers conquered. The issuing power should be taken from the banks and restored to the people, to whom it properly belongs."* Thomas Jefferson

What Thomas Jefferson claimed 200 years ago would happen is happening. I wonder if he was related to Nostradamus.

# NATIONAL DEBT

*"We don't have a trillion dollar debt because we haven't taxed enough; we have a trillion dollar debt because we spend too much."*　　　Ronald Reagan

*"…the principal of spending money to be paid by posterity, under the name of funding, is but swindling futurity on a large scale."*　　　Thomas Jefferson

*"Christmas is the time when kids tell Santa what they want and adults pay for it. Deficits are when adults tell government what they want and their kids pay for it."*
　　　Richard Lamm

United States national debt is a financial culmination of many years of bad fiscal policies, wars, and the borrowing necessary to fund those bad policies and wars. Federal government greed, corruption, and the overwhelming desire of our elected representatives to control us by pampering us are the underlying reasons for our current debt crisis. Liberals believe that any situation they are not in control of is a crisis, but for some incomprehensible reason they don't believe the debt crisis is a crisis. If our national debt situation is not a crisis then I obviously don't know the definition of crisis. I believe if you looked up crisis in a dictionary you would find the words "national debt" somewhere in the definition. The national debt has grown exponentially under the last several presidents including Bush, with each president in turn adding what is, at the time, a significant dollar amount to the debt, or at least it seemed so at the time. Mr. Obama has, in only five years, doubled the national debt that was accumulated by all the previous presidents combined. In other words, Mr. Obama has done in 5 ½ years what it took all the Presidents prior to him to do in 225 years! I'm not sure if my little pea brain can wrap itself around those facts. It becomes even more difficult to comprehend the word trillions when you see it in printed numbers. The zeros never seem to end. When Mr. Obama took office on January 20, 2009 the national debt was less than $10,000,000,000,000 (ten trillion). In just under 5 ½ years of Mr. Obama's fiscal guidance the national debt on June 9, 2014 is in excess of $17,527,558,800,000 (17 ½ trillion). I didn't make those numbers up they come directly from the USA DEBT CLOCK.ORG. There is a lot of very scary but enlightening US financial information at that site. Please be seated when you access it.

Ronald Reagan, George Bush, and Bill Clinton did their parts to increase the national debt and I will make no excuses for them. They own the damage they have done to America's future financial viability. Our elected representatives have sold our futures, our children's futures, and their children's futures trying to make everyone vote for them. The fact remains that every man, woman, and child in American owes $55,077. The fact also remains that each child yet to be born owes the $17 trillion on the books. We have paid over $2.5 trillion in interest on the debt. That dollar amount does not include paying down the $17 trillion principal. That is still owed in its entirety.

The spending has to stop. In the very near future the United States economy is going to go the way of many of the economies in Europe. Greece, Italy, and Spain have had their credit ratings downgraded and are finding it extremely difficult to borrow money to maintain their social programs. Maybe a bad credit rating for America would be a blessing. That would stop the US from going deeper into debt on borrowed money. I'm kidding of course; I know how much damage that would do to the American economy. If the federal government cannot find ways to cut discretionary spending and balance the budget America's financial future is in jeopardy. With the US economy in the slump that it's in, American citizens had to find ways to curb their debt spending and balance their personal budgets. American citizens learn early in life you can't spend more than you make without consequences. It is way beyond time for our federal representatives to realize the same thing. Balance our national budget by not spending more taxpayer money than you can confiscate. It really is as simple as that. The sooner the Washington bureaucrats adopt that type of fiscal policy the sooner our financial healing begins. One of the less than truthful arguments the liberals use against Republicans is that Republicans want to cut spending for the kids and seniors or whatever. Republicans never cut spending on anything. All the Republicans ever try to do is cut the annual increases in spending. The spending stays intact; it just doesn't increase as fast. What a radical concept! I am not normally an alarmist, but I am here to say the healing has got to start immediately or America as we know it, and love it, will become a Third World country dependent on others for our very survival. Scoff at that comment at America's peril.

The United States is staring down the barrel of a financial cannon and the fuse is lit. I don't know when it will go off but it will go off sooner than later. The results will be devastating to the American economy and render it totally unrecognizable; most people say that will never happen; they say it can't happen; they say it never happened before. The people saying that are not the people that lived through the Great Depression of the 1920s and 1930s. The survivors of those economically challenged years have a completely different story. Many of them stood in line for a bowl of soup and a piece of bread. There will be an astonishing amount of subsistence living taking place in the backyards of rural homes and on vacant lots in urban areas. We have become too complacent. We are no longer vigilant to the antics of our elected representative government and we can no longer depend on our pathetic media watchdogs. They are entirely complicit with our government in covering up our looming financial disaster.

I actually have a small way that will start the fiscal responsibility ball rolling. Remember all the poisonous and worthless products like drywall and dog food that Americans purchased from China? Well those Americans filed lawsuits against the Chinese companies that sold those tainted and dangerous products to them. The Americans won the lawsuits and China owes those American citizens billions upon billions of dollars. I say China owes the money because Chinese businesses are literally owned by the Chinese government. The United States owes money to the Chinese government. The Chinese government owes money to American citizens. China says they will never pay the money they owe. Common sense dictates that the American government withholds money owed to China and gives it to the American citizens who won the court cases. That amount of money is then deducted from our debt to China. American citizens will receive a nice windfall. They in turn will spend that windfall and boost the American economy. And last but not least, China's collective conscience will be cleared after having sold dangerous products to America, their best trading partner. If my math is correct after that confusing diatribe, I would call that a win/win/win/win situation: win number one is the US is paying down its debt to China; win number two is the American citizens are receiving their court ordered rewards; win number three is the American citizens are spending the money and boosting the American economy; win number four is the Chinese conscience is cleared. I'm kidding of course, communists have no conscience. That is a brilliant solution to four different calamities. Ouch, I think I dislocated my shoulder patting myself on the back!

# GOVERNMENT FRAUD,
# CORRUPTION *and* GREED

*"Our country is now taking so steady a course as to show by what road it will pass to destruction, to wit by consolidation of power first, and then corruption, it's necessary consequence."*
Thomas Jefferson

**Fraud:** an intentional act of deceiving or misrepresenting in order to induce another to give up something of value.

**Corruption:** inducement to wrong by bribery or other unlawful or improper means.

When citizens lie to a government agency they go to jail. When a politician lies to voters they go into office. When a politician lies in order to obtain something of value, i.e. a citizen's vote, that is the definition of fraud. It simply amazes me that politicians, and many citizens, accept the premise that lying is simply an integral part of politics. It is simply fraud. When a politician tells lies like: "You can keep your doctor"; "You can keep your policy if you like it"; "The cost of your annual premiums will decrease by $2,500"; and uses those statements to justify passing legislation knowing those promises are lies, why is that not fraud? Why does that not, after the fact, make that legislation unlawful and null and void? Lying has always been a part of politics. What we call lying the politicians call "campaign promises". There is no moral or legitimate distinction. We do not have to accept the premise that lying to get elected or to support legislation is "okay because all politicians do it".

When a citizen appears before one of the federal legislative bodies they are put under oath and are sworn to tell the truth. Federal Congressmen take an oath of office that requires them to "defend the Constitution of the United States…and bear true faith and allegiance to the same". Where does lying fit into that oath? When a citizen lies under oath they are committing perjury, a felony punishable by fine and/or imprisonment. Politicians should not be above the laws they force on us!

American taxpayers are no longer perceived by our elected officials as their bosses. To the politicians the American taxpayer has become the enemy to be scoffed at, bullied, taxed, and legislated into submission. Our only purpose in life is to provide the funding that will allow the government to further bully us and make us more dependent on their "generosity". We are not allowed to do things for ourselves. The government tells us how to do it, when we can do it, and ultimately if we can do it. Then they tell us how much we have to pay them to allow us to do it. They pass laws and regulations that they themselves are not required to follow. How in the world did it get to this point? Do we have anyone to blame but ourselves? We have been so happy financially, so busy making a living that we were not paying attention to the details of what they were doing to us under our very noses.

Over many decades of federal legislation all of our constitutional rights have been intentionally, slowly, and methodically eroded away. Over the five years of Mr. Obama we have seen a rapid erosion of our rights. It has not been done slowly and quietly. It has reached a fever pace. No one in our representative government system wants to be called a racist in order to stop it. Does that not show the American citizens how little the Washington establishment cares about "we the people"? Washington would rather allow our great America to be destroyed than to endure some name-calling. That to me is un-American and treasonous. A good analogy of what is happening to our American way of life is to compare it to the way you cook a frog. If you put a frog into boiling water he will jump out of the pot. If you put the frog in cold water and gradually turn up the heat he will not jump out. The frog doesn't realize what is happening to him until it is too late. Ladies and gentlemen, we taxpayers are the frog!

"We the people" are delusional when we claim to maintain the power by voting. Voting has become a mere act to fool the masses into believing we're still in charge. Politicians will promise everything and anything you want in order to get elected. They do as they please once they are firmly in office. They no longer are representatives of the people. They control all of the lawmaking power, the penalty power in the form of the courts, and the police power to enforce it all.

If you don't believe any of this, try walking down the sidewalk of most American cities with a gun. Write a book that is unfavorable to politicians and government and see how fast you get an IRS audit. Don't pay the property taxes on your land and home and see how long the appropriate government agencies let you continue living there. You may think you own it, but you are only renting it from the government. Don't send your hard earned money into the IRS on April 15 and see how quickly they notice that you have not paid for the privilege of working for them for five months of each year.

House Democrat from Virginia, James P. Moron (I'm pretty sure that is the correct spelling of his last name) thinks that his salary of $174,000 per year does not give him enough money to live the lifestyle he deserves. He equates himself and his colleagues with "the board of directors for the largest economic entity in the world" and should be compensated more appropriately by the American taxpayer. On top of their salary, they get funding for staff salaries, office expenses, free transportation, freedom from prosecution for insider trading (addressed later), and much, much more. I read the Washington DC area has the highest rate of wine consumption in the US. Hey Jim, maybe you could cut back on the bar tabs a bit, like the rest of us had to do. The poor people in Washington haven't had a pay increase since 2010. Too damn bad! The taxpayers funding your lifestyle not only haven't had a pay increase, many don't even have jobs anymore because of your laws and regulations. Consider yourself lucky. Try to remain at your current level of salary and benefits in the private sector and see how long you last by doing as little as you do in your current job.

I personally believe our elected officials are vastly overpaid and overcompensated for what we get from them. They produce nothing but suffocating laws and regulations that make it more difficult for the taxpayers to make a decent living. The red tape that they produce is more and more detrimental to the American way of life. The hurdles and hoops they erect are actually barricades at every level of personal and financial achievement. In their minds the red tape represents the ribbons on the Christmas presents they give us. It boggles my mind to think how totally apathetic the Washington establishment is to the plight of the American taxpayer. They sit in their little Beltway utopian bubble completely immune and unaffected by what their detrimental policies are doing to their constituents. I am in constant awe of the corruption, ignorance, naïveté, and complete lack of common sense exhibited on a daily basis by our elected officials in Washington DC.

The Government Accounting Office reported the Pentagon is paying $150 per gallon for "green" jet fuel made from algae. It seems they fall all over themselves trying to come up with the next stupid scheme to waste taxpayer dollars. What's next? Will the taxpayers have to pay $200 per gallon for gasoline made from broccoli for Obama's limo?

Our elected representatives in Washington have been allowed to do insider trading in the stock market for years. They can pass legislation and/or appropriate taxpayer funds to benefit specific companies or industries and before they announce the legislation they can run down and purchase that company stock before the price goes up. That exact same practice has landed many American citizens in jail. When that little tidbit of corruption hit the light of day, they quickly made some legislative changes in the process. You no longer need to wonder how the politicians go into office with a meager net worth, spend a few years legislating, and retire as multimillionaires with full benefits!

Another legislative sleight-of-hand that the Washington elites keep from the public is their process of personal pay increases. For a very long time the method of getting themselves pay increases was for one of them to present it as a bill to be voted on which made it public. To prevent the taxpayers who actually pay for their pay increases from hearing about it, they passed legislation that made pay increases automatic unless someone presented legislation to prevent the increase. Can you imagine a congressman doing that very thing? Now the taxpayers don't have to be burdened with knowing it happens. Pretty crafty, huh?

When the federal government sues an American taxpayer or an American company on behalf of the citizens and wins millions or even billions of dollars, why does the government get to keep the money? Shouldn't that money go to the citizens who were affected? Just wondering.

Obama held a conference at the White House with NFL players to discuss football related concussions. I guess it won't be long before Congress jumps on that cash cow like they did with the tobacco companies. What business was it of Congress to get involved in the use of steroids by baseball players? Should that not be entirely the business of Major League Baseball? The feds sue for a variety of reasons which seldom end up being the reason someone is convicted. The feds can't normally prove the case against someone so they eventually claim the person lied under oath in order to obtain a conviction. Case in point: Martha Stewart was not convicted of insider trading because the feds couldn't prove their case. They decided she lied to them when she claimed she didn't have anything to do with nor remember the securities dealings they accused her of. Martha Stewart went to prison for perjury. Lewis "Scooter" Libby, VP Cheney's Chief of Staff, was brought before the feds in hopes they could convict him of treason for releasing the name of an inactive CIA agent. It turned out to be another typical liberal smear campaign. Scooter denied that he was the first to discuss the name, which turned out to be the truth, but he was convicted of perjury anyway. The feds will commit fraud with no remorse in order to win.

Let's use Harry Reid, Senate leader and liberal icon, as an example of federal corruption. Harry Reid had an impressive early career: George Washington Law School; city attorney; hospital board trustee; Nevada gaming Chairman; Nevada state house; Nevada Lt. Gov.; and United States Senator from Nevada since 1982. Most people believe that Mr. Reid came to Washington as a humble do-gooder lawyer. The truth is, Harry had either been in public office or pursued public office since 1966, directly out of law school. If you look up "career politician" in the dictionary you would see a picture of Harry Reid. It seems a person can't be in public office that length of time without accumulating a vast personal wealth and Harry is no exception. His annual salary as a US Senator is currently $200,000 per year. In 2012 Harry reported a net worth of $2.8-$6.3 million. If you use his top salary of $200,000 per year times 32 years Harry has earned $6.4 million. Harry is not only rich and powerful, he is extremely frugal. He has saved every penny he has earned as US Senator. It would seem that way but Harry has made some very shady land investments in and around Las Vegas over the years that have benefited him, his family, and a few loyal friends. Harry helped appropriate federal funds to build a "bridge-to-somewhere": Harry's property. Needless to say the value of the property soared. Harry readily admits he will help his family in any way possible indicating that a few indiscretions in his 32 year career are not out of the realm of possibility. Harry can be used to illustrate another quick thought about politicians lying to advance their agenda.

Harry made a comment on the Senate floor that Mitt Romney didn't pay federal income taxes. Harry heard that from a friend. Harry was lying and knew he was lying. But he covered himself by saying he didn't know if it was true. It is a federal offense to disclose any taxpayer's IRS information. Both Harry and the friend that disclosed that information should be brought before the Senate, put under oath, and made to testify about the illegally disclosed information. If the story turns out to be true they should both be prosecuted.

Mr. Reid stood up to the podium on the Senate floor recently and stated that all the horror stories about Obamacare are bogus. As Senate Leader, Mr. Reid should take it upon himself to bring those citizen liars in, put them under oath, and force them to tell their lies to the Senate. Make them show their cancellation letters and their premium increases and their higher out-of-pocket costs. Make them prove that their cancer doctors and hospitals can no longer treat them because of Obamacare. Force them to come clean about how they've made up these stories in order to discredit Obamacare. Don't hold your breath for that to happen. Senate Leader Harry Reid is a liar. He has no ethics. He has no morals. He has no conscience. A person cannot possess truthfulness, ethics, morality, or conscience of mind and be a true liberal. None of those four things can be involved in the advancement of the liberal/socialist ideology. If you possess those four attributes you are a conservative.

Another whopper from Harry Reid on the Senate floor was his assertion that 1.6 million Americans lost their jobs because of Obama's sequester. Harry and his liberal cronies swore that the federal budget cut would destroy not only the American economy but the world economy to boot. Two years after the sequester the grand total of jobs lost is one (1). The measly $83 billion trimmed off the budget did not affect the American economy or jobs at all. The reason I call $83 billion measly is because it was trimmed off a $3 trillion budget – $83 billion is precisely .027% of $3 trillion. Don't read that percent wrong: .027% is 27/1000th of a percent.

The reason I used Harry Reid as an example of fraud, corruption, and greed is threefold: first of all Harry Reid, as the Senate Majority Leader, is the most powerful liberal below Barack Obama; secondly, he is loyal to the cause and epitomizes the nastiness of typical liberals; lastly, I used him instead of Nancy Pelosi because he is evil and stupid and Nancy is only stupid. Ouch! I bit my tongue when I said Nancy wasn't evil.

Peaceful civil disobedience en masse will eventually be required to bring this corrupt federal monster under control. I emphasize peaceful now, but it won't remain peaceful for long when the respective government agencies send in their SWAT teams with automatic weapons that we citizens are not allowed to possess. The very sad aspect of that scenario is it will be American on American. Enforcement people will be strong-arming, arresting, and even in some situations, killing their friends, family, and neighbors because they will be ordered to do so. The bureaucrat that will give those orders will be hiding under a desk somewhere in Washington to protect his own butt and political position.

# WASTED TAXPAYER DOLLARS

*"I think we have more machinery of government than is necessary, too many parasites living on the labor of the industrious."* Thomas Jefferson

This will be a lengthy chapter because there is a never-ending list of creative ways the federal government has wasted taxpayer dollars. And let me be completely up front by saying this: some Republicans are equally as guilty as liberals when it comes to wasting taxpayer dollars but the liberals are still the kings. I honestly believe the Washington bureaucrats have federal employees that sit in an office trying to come up with new and improved ways to waste more of our money. Actually, that's exactly how all government bureaucracies operate. When they realize that a specific department, program or agency of the government is unnecessary or particularly wasteful, rather than close that department or agency and save that money, they come up with new ways to preserve that department or agency. And that salvation always involves throwing additional taxpayer money at that agency. There are so many redundant and useless agencies in the federal bureaucracy that it would take an entire book to list them all. I will address a few of the more egregious examples of waste in this book. There is a treasure trove of information about the waste of American taxpayer dollars by our federal bureaucracy. I will reference some of those treasures if you want to do more research on your own. Just keep in mind, the amount of wasteful spending by our federal bureaucrats will be in direct proportion to your increased dislike of those same bureaucrats.

The federal government, or I should say the American taxpayers, owns an unimaginable number of properties and buildings in every state of the union. According to the General Accounting Office of the US government, the US taxpayers own or lease 900,000 buildings but they don't seem to know how many of them are in use and how many of them are vacant. If there are so many we can't keep track of them then we need to put the vacant ones up for sale to the American public and get them back on the tax rolls; let them be revenue producers rather than revenue wasters. Stop inventing new agencies that require a new, fancy building to be built. If the United States cannot survive without that new agency at least house it in one of the existing, vacant buildings we already own. American taxpayers own 302 million acres of property, including 118 million acres of national forest and parks. Stop buying property for parks and conservation set-asides. We do not need to purchase hundreds of thousands of acres of worthless desert for the preservation of some bogus endangered species. One of the more egregious purposes of land grabbing by the current administration is for the sole purpose of stopping energy exploration on that property. Using taxpayer dollars to punish taxpayers sure seems wrong to me, but what do I know?

There are several extremely large federal agencies that are responsible for the largest waste of taxpayer funds. Even though their original purposes were worthy, they have become taxpayer burdens, mostly because of the lack of oversight by their bureaucratic creators but also because of the many lowlife abusers of the programs. They are: the welfare system (food stamps, WIC, and on and on), Medicare, Medicaid, Social Security, the State Department, the Pentagon, the US House and Senate pork barrel projects, just to mention a few. I will present examples of this waste based on information obtained from our very own government's records. All the information about their wasteful ways is public record and allowed to be accessed by anyone. Their fear is that the public occasionally accesses these records. As a side note, because we're talking about waste, pull up the US Congressional Record some time and read about how much time is wasted on a daily basis on exceedingly worthless topics in our congressional chambers. It will turn your stomach. If you don't come away from that little reading experience feeling our federal leaders are massively overpaid for what they do, you have no concept of what is important to the American people and what is absolute political garbage. But I will admit, that on a few occasions, they do actually stumble upon something that is worthy of legislative action.

Our federal welfare system has helped millions upon millions of Americans with their everyday struggle to put a roof over their family's heads and food on the table. Americans are the most compassionate and generous people on the face of the planet. But our welfare system has wasted trillions of taxpayer dollars with abysmal results. Americans in poverty remain at the same percentage of the population now that they were in the 60s when the war on poverty began. The biggest result is also the biggest tragedy: the destruction of the American family unit; mom, dad and the kids. The system has produced what is called "the fatherless family". A single mother can now house, feed, educate, and literally raise her children without the presence of a "breadwinning" father or husband in the household. I would like to give credit to those mothers that have jobs and with the help of taxpayer funds manage to raise those children. On the other hand, ladies, if having children is going to be so much of a financial struggle to raise them without taxpayer funds, don't have them in the first place. As for you fathers, if you have no intention of remaining and helping raise the children, keep it in your pants!

Another abysmal result of the taxpayer funded welfare system in America has been that many have accepted it as a way of life. Generation after generation has come to view American generosity as their given right. The specific programs such as food stamps, WIC, and many others were not originally designed to be used permanently. They were designed as a safety net to help those who fell on hard times and needed short-term public assistance until they were able to fend for themselves again. The original intentions underlying the establishment of the welfare system were honorable. But, as the saying goes, "no good deed goes unpunished". The system was also designed for the use and benefit of Americans. It has become a lifestyle for many non-Americans that are here both legally and illegally. Our open-borders say to any and all comers: "If you can get here by any means, we will feed you, house you, educate you and your children, provide medical care, and give you cash for beer and cigarettes". It is extremely frustrating for me to know that America is playing host, with taxpayer funds, to those who shouldn't be here in the first place. That frustration level continually increases as our level of national debt increases and our economy goes down the drain based on our current national fiscal policies.

Let's talk about food stamps. How many of you know that the food stamp program is funded in the US Department of Agriculture budget? First of all, why is it there? Secondly, the food stamp program accounts for 80% of the Department expenditures. Having to use food stamps at supermarkets was degrading for the users so our hip and technologically savvy federal government decided to discontinue the food stamps and issue what is called Electronic Benefit Transfer or EBT cards. They look like a normal credit card or debit card but don't carry the same stigma for the user as do food stamps. Each month the cardholder has additional taxpayer funds electronically authorized to the card. As with all federal programs the cards are easily abused. In the past people could sell their food stamps at a discounted rate to obtain cash for use other than buying groceries. With the EBT card, the abuse is even easier. The cards can be used anywhere that you can swipe a credit card and for anything you want. The cards are being used for gambling in Las Vegas, at liquor stores, at strip clubs, and anywhere else, for purposes other than groceries to feed a family. The abuse is rampant and very costly to the American taxpayer. The US Department of Agriculture uses taxpayer funds from the program to help people get on the food stamp program. That help is not limited to American citizens. The USDA advertises the use of American food stamps in Mexico. What does it say about a government that spends trillions of taxpayer dollars to get people on a program that makes them more dependent on taxpayer money but doesn't spend a dime trying to help them get off that program? Another of those rhetorical questions, right?

"Obama phones" is a recent example of the waste of taxpayer funds. Not only was the original taxpayer purchase of phones wasteful, the program was and is massively abused by its participants. There have been, and will continue to be, examples of people being given access to phones that are not qualified to receive a phone based on the criteria set by the program itself. Worse yet, they were allowed access to several phones. The bulk of the American people already had cell phones when this program went into effect. The only possible motive for establishing this free cell phone giveaway was to buy votes for the liberals. Please find an adult within the federal bureaucracy that determines this program is a bad idea and possibly unlawful in the eyes of the Federal Election Commission, and put an end to it. I'm not asking for anyone to be prosecuted because if we did something about this we would have to prosecute every politician in America. Republicans are nearly as guilty as liberals of vote buying schemes whether they are the party in power or not. I would only like to end the waste of taxpayer dollars.

There have not been any more glaring examples of taxpayer funds being wasted than by Mr. Obama on his donor's bogus "green energy" companies and their projects. Billions upon billions of taxpayer dollars went to companies that manufactured components for solar or wind generation systems or some other "pie-in-the-sky" green scheme. The waste of the money was bad enough but the fact that each of the company owners was a big Obama donor also puts it on the lengthy Obama scandal list. Had this happened under a Republican president, there would be no end to the Congressional and FEC investigations. If not for Fox News and Drudge Report, the American public would have no idea this was happening. I cover this in a little more detail in the Obama Scandal chapter.

Federal contractors are constantly being caught overcharging the US taxpayers for substandard work but seldom get prosecuted because they are some bureaucrat's business partner, friend or nephew. But you can imagine the number of contractors working in the shadows that overcharge; do shoddy work; or bill for work that they didn't complete. I didn't do the research that would reveal the contractors that did outstanding work; brought the contracted project in on time and on budget and maybe even under; but they are out there. The sad fact is: no one ever reports on the good guys. The federal contracting bureaucracy is so massive it appears to be impossible to oversee all of the contract work in progress. The truth is, no check should be cut to a contractor without an inspection of the work. If the inspector in charge signs off on the incomplete or shoddy work the inspector should be looking for a new career path after a brief stay in federal prison. If it were their own money would they not be more diligent?

I have a construction background both as a contractor and an inspector. I have never seen a contract in the private sector that didn't hold the contractor to a specific scope of work and the owner to a specific schedule of payments based on the timely completion of that work. On large projects there would be contingency funds available in the project budget that would handle most all surprises. Additions and/or corrections could be made to any portion of the contract with change orders approved by all parties. Change orders are sometimes necessary but are to be avoided whenever possible. If the owner presented the scope of the project properly to the contractor and the contractor returned a legitimate bid for that project based on the owner's scope of work then there would be little need for change orders or accessing the contingency funds. There was also a penalty clause that stated if the contractor did not complete the project on the agreed-upon date the contractor would be charged a daily financial penalty until completion. If the contractor misjudged the cost of the project or materials, he better get his wallet out because he's going to pay for the additional costs. It doesn't work that way in government contracting. Government contracting standards are considerably more lax than in the private sector. In government contracting the rule of thumb is this: "If you run out of time, Mr. Contractor, we will give you more time. If you run out of money, Mr. Contractor, we will give you more taxpayer money". I believe there are two reasons for the inevitable "over budget" costs of government projects: 1. They are not spending their own money; 2. A portion of the overrun money comes back to them in campaign donations.

If you want good examples of wasted taxpayer money you need look no further than nearly every road, subway tunnel, bridge, or transit rail built in the large cities. Every project comes in millions or even billions of dollars over budget. Many projects take additional months and some cases years over the allotted timeframe for completion. A prime example of government incompetence resulting in large-scale wasted taxpayer dollars is Boston's Central Artery/Tunnel Project or more affectionately called the "Big Dig". The purpose of the project was to move a major highway through the heart of the city from the surface into a 3 ½ mile tunnel. Construction started in 1991 and was completed in 2006. It was originally scheduled for completion in 1998. It took an additional eight years to complete. The original estimated cost was $2.8 billion. The cost at completion was $14.6 billion. But there are estimates floating around that will put the actual cost at $22 billion. Shoddy work, tunnel leaks, some original design flaws, and the use of substandard materials all contributed to the astronomical cost overruns and delays in completion. Having taken 15 years to complete and considering population increases the tunnel was probably undersized by the time it was finished.

Read the 2008 *Pig Book* by Citizens Against Government Waste. The top 3 pork spenders were ranking Republican members of the Senate Appropriations Committee. Don't ever again doubt why it is important to Congressmen to be on committees in Washington. I have no problem with our elected officials bringing home taxpayer dollars for their states. They are there to represent their constituents specifically but also to support what is good for the entire nation. But when they support projects that waste taxpayer dollars solely for the purpose of getting the voters of their state to vote for them again, they have crossed the line. So the liberals don't feel left out of this conversation, I'll make a couple comments about Virginia Senator Robert Byrd. He managed to nudge the Republicans off the trough on many occasions. He took so much federal taxpayer money home to his state they named half of the government buildings and three fourths of the roads in the state after him. (Okay, the numbers are exaggerated but there are a lot named after him.) Very generous tributes to a past KKK recruiter, but then I digress. With all due respect to the departed, he did very well for his state, but I assure you, when an official sends that much money home there will be large sums of that taxpayer money spent on wasteful projects.

On a smaller scale of wasted taxpayer funds, but waste nonetheless, would be National Public Radio, and the Public Broadcasting System. NPR and PBS outlived their usefulness many, many years ago. They originated in 1970 and were designed to be public announcement systems to keep the American public more informed about supposedly nonpartisan news and issues. Both the radio and the TV stations receive a large amount of funding from unwilling American taxpayers via the federal government. NPR wastes approximately $22 million of taxpayer funds. PBS wastes around $450 million of taxpayer funds. The balance of their funding comes from willing taxpayer donations. Each time someone calls for their defunding by the taxpayers, the supporters claim the loss of taxpayer funding would not have a large effect on their programming. If that's the case, then why not give it a try. Call their bluff and defund them. Liberals are the only supporters of the two stations because from their inception their programs were left-leaning propaganda. Their hosts have always been, and with liberal support always will be, hard-core leftists. Let them compete on the open market just as all other radio and television affiliates have to do. Liberals are in favor of the "Fairness Doctrine" so why don't we try it out on PBS and NPR? Since they are taxpayer funded they should be the stations that the liberals use as guinea pigs to try out new ways to stifle our First Amendment's Freedom of Speech. The two stations would be required to program equal time for conservative views that they allot for liberal views. If Jarl Mohn, President of NPR; a donor to Obama, the Democratic National Committee, and the ACLU; had to allot time for conservative views on his airwaves he would undoubtedly quit. If liberal media icons Bill Moyer and Gwen Ifill of PBS were required to adhere to that doctrine of equal time I believe I would probably hear their heads explode from my house! Here's a quick side note: Paula Kerger, current president of PBS, takes home a salary of $632,233 annually. Paula also claims federal funding is miniscule to their budget. That being the case, they should be able to stay in existence without taxpayer funding.

The National Endowment for the Arts was established in 1965 during President Johnson's New Deal era. It wastes $150 million annually. It lowers the standards of art by subsidizing lousy artists rather than make them compete in an open market. There is one project that always comes to my mind but I refuse to call it art. I apologize up front for this, but the name of the piece is "Piss Christ". It is without a doubt one of the most disgusting displays of garbage ever created by a human being! It is a picture of a crucifix in a jar of the "artist's" urine. Art aficionados claim the beauty of art is in the eyes of the beholder and the heart of the artist. This beholder still considers it garbage. I hold the black-hearted artist, Andres Serrano, and also the person or persons responsible for paying him $5,000 of taxpayer funds, in complete and utter contempt. I've said it, I meant it, and I will not take it back! All I have done to them is voice my opinion about their lack of judgment. Imagine what would happen to that individual had he placed a picture of the Islamic god in a jar of urine. His body would not arrive in hell with his head attached! Another example of an offensive project would be one that displays the American flag in a toilet. I understand that there is a sizable number of Americans that are not offended by that, but they should be. The majority of the taxpayer funds wasted by NEA are for decidedly left-leaning projects.

I have never understood the need for federal employees to have government issued credit cards. There cannot possibly be a need for any goods or services that would require payment in advance with a credit card. Have the feds never heard of purchase orders? The purchase order is approved by someone, hopefully, who has a legible signature and can be held accountable for each specific purchase; no rubberstamps; no "auto pen" or whatever they're called, should be allowed. The misuse of taxpayer funds should be cause for immediate termination, prosecution, and restoration of funds. That is how the system works in private business and government employees should be held to the same standards. Taxpayers fund credit card abuse by civil servants to the tune of tens of billions of dollars each year. The cards are used for personal purchases including, but not limited to, airfare, gambling, prostitution, jewelry, electronic equipment including computers, and any other item the cardholder chooses to purchase. The government knows who the abusers are but in most cases will not fire them or prosecute them. They don't even require the money to be returned. Our U.S. Congress refuses to hold anyone accountable simply because they themselves and their staff members are equal abusers of taxpayer funds.

I'm going to make a couple more bigoted and biased remarks. The federal welfare system in its entirety was developed by the federal government and funded by confiscated American taxpayer money. The bulk of it was developed by the bleeding heart liberals and supported by naïve Republicans. I remarked earlier that the programs were designed as a leg up rather than a legacy. The problem with the welfare system, as has always been the case, is the fact that it is completely dependent on taxpayers. With the economy in its downward spiral and the loss of millions of American jobs, the funding of the welfare programs is being pressed to its limits. With fewer Americans working there is less revenue to fund these programs. We are at present, very near the point where there are more "takers" than there are "makers". When we top-over that balance point the very existence of the United States of America is in jeopardy.

Mr. Clinton signed some very good welfare reform legislation in the mid-90s under pressure from the Republicans. Some of those "tough love" laws resulted in a very large number of welfare recipients again taking care of themselves. Mr. Obama, by executive order or some other illegal means, rescinded some portions of that law. There's something to be said for receiving your own paycheck and the self-respect that goes along with it.

Mr. Obama took away some of that self-respect and again replaced it with dependency.

I want to dredge up a few old ideas that should be imposed on welfare recipients that are capable of physical work. There are millions of Americans that receive a legitimate paycheck for cleaning parks, streets, sidewalks and anything else that needs cleaned. There is no stigma to having that type of job. Why can't welfare recipients be required to do some of those jobs in order to receive their checks? Is it because the liberals feel it would be too demeaning to their voters? But wasn't it a liberal administration that set up the WPA program (Works Progress Administration) in 1939 to put unemployed Americans to work at those very types of jobs? Why was it good policy back then and demeaning now? Most insurance companies require private companies to randomly drug test their employees to ensure the safety and well-being of all employees. If an employee fails a drug test their employment is normally immediately terminated. Why should welfare recipients not be required to do random drug testing to continue to receive their checks? Just some food for thought: If liberals are all about fairness and leveling the playing field why not be consistent?

# PRESIDENTIAL SCANDALS

*"When a man assumes a public trust he should consider himself a public property."*
                                                                    Thomas Jefferson

**John F. Kennedy:**
1.  Failed CIA attempt to invade Cuba in 1961, "Bay of Pigs'.
2.  Alleged affair with Marilyn Monroe.

**Lyndon Johnson:**
1.  Power-hungry drunk.
2.  Escalated the Vietnam conflict that got 58,000 American boys killed.
3.  His "New Deal Society" was the basis for the modern day liberal ideology and the out-of-control welfare system.

**Richard Nixon:**
1.  The purpose of the Watergate break-in in 1972 was to obtain liberal policy secrets; Nixon was not involved in the original planning but was caught lying and covering up the act; resigned to prevent his full impeachment.
2.  He was a political bully; he was not opposed to using illegal methods such as office bugging or the threat of IRS investigations to intimidate his opponents.

**Gerald Ford:**
1.  He continued Nixon policies.
2.  He was in charge over a severe economic downturn.
3.  He pardoned Nixon.
4.  He couldn't stop hitting people with golf balls.

**Jimmy Carter:**
1.  Everything he did was wrong for America.
2.  Created the Department of Education and the Department of Energy; both bad federal agencies.
3.  Single-handedly initiated modern day terrorism by allowing the mullahs to take over Iran.

4. Failed attempt to rescue American hostages that were taken because of his Iran policies.

5. His weak Middle Eastern policies signaled to Russia the US would not interfere with their invasion of Afghanistan.

6. Presided over a terrible economy based on an energy shortage because of his Middle Eastern policies.

7. Gave away the Panama Canal.

**Ronald Reagan:**

1. The Iran-contra scandal was brought on due to a liberal Congress trying to protect the communist leader in Nicaragua.

2. Several Department of Housing and Urban Development officials were caught giving Reagan campaign donors housing bids.

3. Some of Reagan's aides were convicted of lobbying after they left government service; I don't think that's illegal now.

4. A very large savings and loan collapse bailout costing American taxpayers $160 billion; sound familiar?

5. His administration was marred by scandals, investigations, indictments, or convictions of 138 officials.

6. Granted amnesty to 1.5 million illegal aliens.

**George H. W. Bush:**

1. Tried to provide cover for his son Neil who was involved in the savings-and-loan collapse.

2. Guaranteed the American people he would not raise taxes and then did.

**Bill Clinton:**

1. His sex scandals were common knowledge as far back as his governorship in Arkansas and too numerous to mention here. The only question I have is: When he lied and perjured himself about Monica Lewinsky, why did he not have enough integrity to resign like Richard Nixon did over Watergate? I resented the fact that he did what he did in the American people's Oval Office.

2. He allowed American military technology to be given to China for campaign donations.

3. He used the IRS to harass and intimidate his political opponents and media detractors.

4. Bill and Hillary both were involved in shady investment and billing practices at the Whitewater Law Firm in Arkansas.

## George W. Bush:

1. The big faux pas of course was that Bush "lied" about weapons of mass destruction being an excuse to invade Iraq. In his defense, every liberal leader in the United States agreed that Saddam Hussein had WMD and the US should do everything in its power to take those weapons away from him. Bush was given virtually unanimous congressional consent to invade. But after all these years of "Bush lied people died" the new headline is the radical Iraqi Islamic terrorists (ISIS) that are taking back Iraq have now gained control of Saddam's weapons of mass destruction including sarin gas stockpiles and nuclear materials; the very sarin gas that never existed. Someone may owe Bush and Cheney an apology. Don't hold your breath until that happens.

2. The Abu Ghraib prison controversy was a big to do about nothing more sinister than a few ignorant soldiers treating prisoners no worse than some college fraternity hazing; get a life people.

3. Bush firing US Attorneys and replacing them with his picks was the standard practice of every president before him.

4. Guantánamo Bay prisoners are treated better than the US soldiers that guard them.

5. "Waterboarding" is not torture. The questioning of prisoners does not cross over into torture until marks are left on the body or blood is drawn. Pouring water in someone's face is an old time technique devised to wake them up from unconsciousness or a drunken stupor. Beheading is torture.

## Barack H. Obama:

1. The billions of taxpayer dollars given to his personal donors companies to promote "green" projects.

2. Lying to ensure Obamacare would become law.

3. Continued lying to ensure Obamacare would remain a law.

4. Continually changing established law (Obamacare) for personal and liberal political gains.

5. "Fast and Furious" gun-running to the Mexican drug cartels resulting in the deaths of at least two border patrol agents; there will be no justice brought against the Obama administration cover-up using Attorney General Holder's Department of Justice because he is also neck-deep in the treacherous activity.

6. The recent sequester that Obama claimed would destroy the American economy, starve children, kill old people, and effectively shut down government was originally his idea. The Republicans called his bluff and still got blamed for damage that never happened.

7. Obama has continued to bypass Congress and ignore currently established laws to allow illegals to cross into the United States unimpeded and in some respects aided.

8. Obama's unrelenting cover and support for Islamic terrorism allowed four American heroes to be murdered in Benghazi; he continues to impede a congressional investigation that would very easily prove his administration's culpability in the tragedy.

9. His use of the IRS to silence and intimidate his political foes has far out-shadowed even Bill Clinton's use of the IRS for the same purposes. No prosecution expected here either.

10. Veterans Administration scandal has been brought to the forefront because of recent provable deaths of veterans at the hands of the VA's lack of care. Obama used what he considered George Bush's lack of concern for the veterans as a campaign topic and promised to correct the many discrepancies in the handling of the VA.

I heard about Ted Cruz's "The Legal Limit Report Number 4; The Obama Administrations Abuses of Power" which lists 76 illegal actions that Obama has taken by executive order. The title alone beckons me to read the report. I purposely have not read it for fear that our like-minded thinking may give some folks the false impression that I have plagiarized his work. I will read it after this book is in print.

Since The Obama Administration scandals are current and directly in our faces at this point I will make some additional comments on several of the situations. The Obama scandals are coming so fast that my list will be "old news" by the time this book is out. After all, Obama has two and half years left in his term, I don't believe he will be able to help himself.

So far there have been about 20 "green" energy companies that have received well over $5 billion in taxpayer funds from the Obama slush fund.

There are two interesting points about those 20 companies: all of the companies have already failed or are in some stage of bankruptcy; 80% of the 20 companies and their owners donated to Obama's campaign coffers. This is by no means the entire list of companies that Obama has given taxpayer funding to for "green" energy research or product development. These are only the companies that have failed so far. Several of these companies were not even American companies and even more on the list sent taxpayer dollars overseas for research and product development. You'll recognize the names Solyndra, SunPower, First Solar, Fisker Automotive and Sun Trust of America. Some of these companies received taxpayer dollars even though Obama was aware they were failing. This paragraph of information made the "scandal" chapter rather than the "government waste" chapter because of the large percentage of Obama donors receiving taxpayer funds. Can anyone say "quid pro quo" or "impeachable offense"? This is the only "pay-as-you-go" program that Obama has ever supported.

The established law that is Obamacare is being revised again by Obama. He is requesting the insurance companies maintain lower premiums prior to the 2014 and 2016 election cycles. He has assured the companies he will cover their losses with taxpayer funds. It seems strange that liberals would request favors from the very insurance providers that they have condemned in the past as the evil perpetrators of America's unjust and expensive healthcare system. But then again when you're working with no conscience the sky is the limit.

The Obama administration continues to claim that their Operation Fast and Furious program of gunrunning was no more than a continuation of a George Bush program. That is false. The "gun-walking" program initiated under George Bush was stopped by George Bush because it was difficult to trace weapons into Mexico which made it extremely dangerous. Operation Fast and Furious started nine months into Obama's administration. It was begun as a way to give American guns to the Mexican drug cartel, catch them with the guns, and then claim we needed additional gun control in America to prevent that from happening. It was a very dangerous and sneaky way to initiate a crisis that would give Obama a better argument in the gun control debate. It went beyond sneaky; it became deadly for two US border patrol agents and an untold number of civilians who were murdered with the guns.

Obama's war on guns continues to get more effective. The federally operated Federal Deposit Insurance Corporation (FDIC) is forcing bankers to categorize gun retailers and manufacturers with drug paraphernalia stores and porn shops so they can drop them as high credit risks. That will effectively prevent them from getting a line of credit or processing on-line sales. All of this is being done behind closed doors without congressional involvement by "the most transparent presidency in history".

I know I can't pin this recent "crisis" of all the illegal minor children crossing our southern border directly on Mr. Obama but he is ultimately responsible for what is happening. Our inquisitive US Congress is asking why we are having such a large surge. I will tell them: Obama flagrantly disregarded immigration laws and promised amnesty to his "Dream Kids" making their parents bold enough to take advantage of our unprotected borders. But let's give additional credit where credit is due. John Boehner and the establishment Republican leadership have promised amnesty would happen in 2014. Did they honestly believe that no one below our southern border was listening? Everyone seems surprised that this is happening when in reality it was the goal. It was, of course, all orchestrated. Republicans were dragging their feet on amnesty so, as Rahm Emmanuel would recommend: create a crisis that will force Congress to act immediately. If the administration did not know this was going to take place how did they know immediately how many children had already crossed the border? How did they already have a prediction that an additional 140,000 illegal children would cross the border in 2015? Why were there buses at ready to disperse the children and abandoned buildings all around the US prepped and ready to receive them? This is all another example of the federal government forcing something on the American taxpayers that we don't want and can't afford. I am insulted that they believe we can't see through their lying and corruption. What it finally proves is the fact that the liberals don't give a rat's rear end about children. Who in their sane mind would turn those children from El Salvador, Guatemala, and Honduras loose hoping they could get here without adult help? Considering Mexico has severe criteria for entering their southern border, how did 60,000 minor children as young as three years old get into and across Mexico without anyone noticing? "We the people" are no longer in charge of our destiny. We are merely pawns on the federal government's chessboard and just as the chess pieces are eliminated or retained at their pleasure so are we.

After a couple years of Congress trying to investigate Obama's IRS scandal there has remained nothing but lies and cover-up from the administration. The interim, and extremely condescending, IRS Commissioner, John Koskinen, appeared before Congress recently and said that "further investigation into the IRS scandal would be a monumental waste of taxpayer funds". To some extent I actually agree with him. No matter what they eventually uncover no one in the IRS or the Obama administration will be held accountable. Congress does not have the intestinal fortitude to pursue prosecutions on anyone even if Obama and Attorney General Eric Holder would permit it. In a recent interview Mr. Obama stated there was "not even a smidgen of corruption" in the IRS scandal. In order to back that up all of the e-mails from Lois Lerner and the other six top executives in charge at the IRS for the period in question have been irretrievably lost. Only the e-mails those seven people sent to the White House, the Justice Department, Congress, and the Securities Exchange Commission were lost. Their IT people say that not only were they lost but they took special care to destroy the respective hard drives of the computers in question. I'll bet the National Security Agency (NSA) and/or treasonous Mr. Snowden have all of those emails! Why are so many coincidences so obviously not coincidences? They are lying to us, they know they are lying to us, and not only do they not care but they do it with ease.

After 5 ½ years into Obama's administration not only has he not done anything to alleviate the despicable behavior of the VA, he has allowed the situation to deteriorate further. I cannot stress enough the disgust and disappointment I have for the American government over the treatment our veterans receive at our Veterans Administration hospitals and clinics. It is so disheartening to know that our military personnel are sent into harm's way and our government has so little regard for them that they treat them as if they are a burden when they return home wounded; physically or mentally or both. How ironic that our elected officials sit in climate controlled offices and disrespect the very people they send to fight in the worst climates around the world. How ironic that our elected officials are allowed to use the best medical facilities in America for themselves and their families while providing the worse facilities for our fighting men and women and their families. This situation would be cleaned up immediately if our legislators were required to use the VA facilities for themselves and their families. After completely screwing up the healthcare of a few million American veterans, this same government wants complete control of all American health care. Maybe our military personnel should be allowed to unionize because no union in the United States would allow this treatment of their members by anyone including the federal government.

Obama has repeatedly stated that Al Qaeda has been defeated. Worldwide terrorism is on the rise under Obama's leadership and shows no sign of lessening. Half of the Middle East is burning; the gunfire and explosions never cease. Children are being murdered in Israel. The ISIS is on the verge of reclaiming Iraq. Putin is edging closer to an outright takeover of Ukraine. Iran is funding the Al Qaeda rebels in Iraq and Syria with the hopes of adding those two countries to their caliphate. In the meantime, all that has taken the heat off Iran and freed them to complete a nuclear weapon; which I believe is closer to realization than the Obama administration will freely admit. Mr. Obama's foreign policy of "leading from behind" just doesn't seem to have made the grade.

If Obama, Hillary, Hagel, and the rest of his administration had made at least some effort to help the ambassador and the three other American heroes who died in Benghazi they wouldn't be in the mess they are in now. Had they come clean about the incident immediately and apologized and actually followed through with his threat to bring the people responsible to justice, he would be a hero instead of a zero. But they resorted to lies and cover-ups for political purposes: he had to prevent the truth about his incompetence coming out just prior to his upcoming presidential election; he had to cover up the fact that Al Qaeda was not defeated as he had previously bragged.

It's all these things that cause the favorability ratings of Barack Obama to be in the 30 percentile range. It's all these things that cause a favorability rating of Congress to be in single digits. A recent Public Policy Polling survey showed Congress had a favorability rating of 9%. According to the survey Americans were more favorable to being stuck in traffic, having head lice, having a colonoscopy or a root canal than they were to liking what Congress is doing at this point in history. It makes a person want to wish each of those calamities on some certain individuals in Washington.

# OBAMA

*"I have never been able to conceive how any rational being could propose happiness to himself from the exercise of power over others."* Thomas Jefferson

*"All tyranny needs to gain a foothold is for people of good conscience to remain silent."* Thomas Jefferson

Is this the chapter that will get me labeled a racist and also get me an IRS audit? Let's address some things up front. I do not hate black people in general, and I do not hate Barack Obama specifically. It might even be a hoot to play golf with him if he could find time in his busy schedule to play golf. I have to assume that Obama's Kenyan relatives are decent people, although I'm not too thrilled with some of his white ancestors. My beef with Obama is limited entirely to his socialist-leaning policies as president and his complete disregard for the plight of the American taxpayer. I will feel exactly the same way about Hillary if she becomes president. Opps, I just revealed my sexist side. What is particularly sad is the fact that his time as president will have such a detrimental impact on our American way of life. Following liberal logic, Mr. Obama cannot be held personally responsible for any of his actions. It was the way he was brought up by a socialist mother and like-minded grandparents. His mentors from a very early age were socialists. As noted by him in his autobiographies those were the types of people that he gravitated towards as he become the man he is today. "Rules for Radicals", written by Saul Alinsky, must be his bible. Everyone he surrounds himself with to this day is a politically left-leaning, anti-American socialist. You don't have to take my word for that, just do some simple research on the backgrounds of all his cabinet heads and czars. No one in his clique believes in "American Exceptionalism". To the last individual, all believe the United States of America was conceived illegitimately at the expense of the rest of the world's population. According to their way of thinking the United States owes the world its very existence. The best way for us to make amends is to spread America's wealth and power to the rest of the world to the extent the United States becomes a third world dictatorship under Mr. Obama's care. Let the racist hate-mongering begin! But hold your horses folks; I'm just getting warmed up.

I'm going to go into a little more depth concerning Mr. Obama's past and present socialist associations. Of course his first and primary association was with his socialist mother, and that style of upbringing was continued on when his mother's parents, Stanley and Madelyn Dunham, took over as his surrogate parents. The next major influence in Mr. Obama's life was Frank Marshall Davis, a self-avowed socialist/communist. Mr. Davis mentored teenager Barack in Hawaii in the socialist/Marxist way of life. Vernon Jarrett of Chicago was also a communist and a good friend of Mr. Davis'. Vernon's daughter-in-law, Valerie, is the top Obama senior adviser at the White House. I honestly believe that Valerie and Michelle are co-president. The entire socialist, communist, Chicago, and Hawaii connection specifically speaks to Obama's political upbringing and explains his socialist-leaning style of governing. Obviously, the lessons have had a lasting effect. The socialist indoctrination was well received by Barack and followed him into his college years where the socialist ideas were completely cemented in his psyche. His mentors directly after college were all socialists as well. Self-avowed terrorists Bill Ayers and Bernadine Dohrn took Barack under their wings and introduced him to Chicago's socialist crowd and their many anti-American causes. He spent several years advancing those causes as a community organizer for organizations such as ACORN, a front for felonious liberals hell-bent on voter fraud. As a "clean, articulate" young black man (Joe Biden's words, not mine) Barack was destined for a bright political future and was well received by the Chicago socialist elites, giving him access to campaign cash and voters. His political debut happened in Bill Ayers and Bernadine Dohrn's Chicago living room.

Another large influence on Mr. Obama's life was his pastor of 20 years, Jeremiah Wright. He was Obama's spiritual mentor and even presided over Barack and Michelle's wedding. The Obama family members were frequent attendees and faithful followers of Reverend Wright's teachings. The world beyond Chicago had heard very little about Reverend Wright until he and his teachings were revealed as a result of Obama's presidential candidacy. I believe I would be safe in saying that Reverend Wright never had any intention for the recordings of him at the pulpit to be made public. Jeremiah Wright stood up at the pulpit in front of his congregation, probably including the Obama family, and stated: "Not God bless America, but God damn America". I apologize for printing all the words but it was necessary for its complete impact. Obama had to believe, deep in his soul, what Jeremiah Wright was saying or he wouldn't have sat through that type of sermon for 20 years. Don't think for a minute that sermon topic was an isolated event. You know by just those few words, and his tone, that Jeremiah Wright is an America hater and presides over a like-minded congregation. Obama left Jeremiah Wright's church reluctantly, and only after determining that his association with Jeremiah Wright and his church would be extremely detrimental to his political future. Once Mr. Obama is out of office I would not be surprised in the least to hear he quietly returned to the church. "Birds of a feather flock together."

Something that has irritated me from the very beginning of Mr. Obama's campaign was his continual promise that his administration would be the most open and transparent administration in US history. I have yet to see that transparency. It has been the complete opposite. Since the beginning of Mr. Obama's administration the only transparency we have witnessed is in the illegality and corruption of his administration. It seems there is a lot of closed-door scheming going on and the public only hears about it when someone passes a note under the door. The problem is that even when the note is leaked the mainstream media will not report on it for fear it might make Mr. Obama look bad. Enough said about that here. There will be an entire chapter on Mr. Obama's MSM. Mr. Obama has effectively sealed the records of his entire life. We don't know anything about his adoption by Mr. Soetoro or his years in Indonesia, or his citizenship status during that period of his life. We don't know his course study and grades at Occidental, or his course study and grades at Oxford University, or his course study and grades at Harvard University nor anything about his tenure as the head of the Harvard Law Review. We know nothing about his student status and how or who paid for his schooling. George Bush released his college records and they were scrutinized, picked apart, and laughed at right down to the "C" he received on his report card. Personal military service records were released by Mr. Bush and to no one's surprise the liberals criticized his honorable service. Mr. Obama has spent millions of dollars on attorneys to prevent that same data about him from being made public. I've heard it said that the only reason a person would hide information is because he has something bad to hide. I'm just saying. His autobiographies discuss generalities of those years but none of the pertinent details. About the only parts of Mr. Obama's history that he couldn't hide were his life as a community organizer and his tenure as an Illinois senator. None of those years are flattering to Mr. Obama. As a community organizer he ingratiated himself with the socialist crowd he worked for. He was prodded and supported into public office. In the Illinois Senate he did two things: pass legislation to end the lives of babies who survived abortions, and..... I can't come up with the second thing because nearly every time he was there to vote, he voted "present". He was not available to vote at all the last couple years as a senator in Illinois because those were the years he was busy campaigning for president. Those above things were Mr. Obama's complete list of qualifications to be President of the United States, twice! But paraphrasing Mr. Obama's own words: "You didn't do that on your own; someone else did it for you".

Now that we have had him for over 5 ½ years, I am hard-pressed to think of any good policies or legislation that Barack Obama has put forward that has been beneficial for the American people. Santa Claus giveaways don't count because those are simply vote buying schemes. His signature legislation, Obamacare, is the worst federal law to be forced on the American public since the IRS was established. I won't go into depth with Obamacare here because it deserves its own chapter.

One of the latest ill-conceived moves by the Obama administration is to allow the current "gatekeeper" of the global internet, Internet Corporation for Assigned Names and Numbers, to be taken over by an entity other than the United States; including the United Nations, or any other country of the world. That gives the United Nations and all the countries ruled by dictators and thugs the opportunity to control the global Internet system. Communist China has stepped forward and is making a concerted effort to take control of the international Internet. That would allow them to tax the use of the internet and impose any form of censorship on anyone, at any time, for any reason. Is that a nice guy giving others the chance to play in the sandbox or is it simply another example of Mr. Obama's intentional damage to the American economy?

I don't know about the rest of you but I am tired of the Obama administration using George Bush as its scapegoat for everything. I'm guessing here of course, but if Obama made a bad shot on the golf course it would somehow be Bush's fault. After 5 ½ years of Obama's presidency he should, at some point, except responsibility for what is happening around him. Here are some interesting comparisons of eight years of George Bush and just over five years of Barack Obama:

1. The number of Americans on food stamps has increased 70% under Obama. There will be a record 46.8 million Americans enrolled in the Supplemental Nutrition Assistance Program (SNAP) in 2014.

2. The national average price for regular gasoline when Bush left office in January 2009 was just over $1.80 per gallon. The national average price for regular gasoline on May 20, 2014 under Obama was $3.65 per gallon.

3. According to the Bureau of Labor Statistics overall grocery prices have increased by 2.6% each year for five years (December 2007 through December 2012). Five years × 2.6% per year equals 13% increase. Hogwash, I do the shopping for our household of two and what was $75 per week for groceries five years ago is now $110 or more per week. That is at least a 47% increase over five years.

4. National debt when George Bush took office in January 2001 was $5.6 trillion. The national debt when George Bush left office in January 2009 was $10.6 trillion. That is an increase of $5 trillion over eight years. The national debt as of May 20, 2014 is $17.5 trillion representing an increase of $6.9 trillion in just over five years under Obama. If Obama remains on the same unsustainable spending spree he is currently on he will easily increase the national debt in his eight years by $10 trillion bringing the debt total when he leaves office to $20.6 trillion. $20,600,000,000,000; that is a lot of zeros!

5. This is going to seem petty to some but I'm going to mention that Mr. Obama has played over 160 rounds of golf in his 5 ½ years as president. Mr. Obama has never let a presidential duty interfere with his golf game. Mr. Bush dropped golf after invading Iraq and gave this explanation: "I don't want some mom, whose son may have recently died, to see the commander-in-chief playing golf". Obviously, that thought has never crossed Mr. Obama's mind. Mr. Bush has also defended Mr. Obama playing golf because even the president needs a pressure relief. Now the golf playing does seem petty. The real comparison between the two presidents is the fact that Mr. Bush has always been and will remain a "class act". Obama didn't play much golf before becoming president; I guess he has more time on his hands now. After 160 rounds you would think he could play 18 holes in less than five hours!

Obama has added more national debt in a little over five years than all the presidents preceding him combined. The national debt did not equal the $6.9 trillion Obama increase until a couple years into George Bush's presidency. It took the 43 presidents before Obama 225 years to produce the debt that Obama will produce in eight years. That intentional increase will very well be the end of the American economy in particular and the American society in general.

The Obama administration and his liberal friends claim we are in a recovery. I can't speak for anyone but myself, but I honestly don't see it. Whether Obama wants to admit it or not he owns the bad economy; the incompetent and embarrassing roll-out of Obamacare; the dangerous results of his foreign policies; and the doubling of our national debt in just five years of his leadership. Each time a new administration secret is leaked or a new administration scandal is revealed Mr. Obama claims complete ignorance of the topic. He only learns about it through the news at the same time the American public learns about it. It reminds me of Sgt. Schultz on the old TV show Hogan's Heroes: "I know nothing". As the most powerful man on the planet and the leader of the free world, Mr. Obama is required to know everything. If what he says is true and he is uninformed or ill-informed by his staff and cabinet heads he needs to immediately fire the incompetent people. Maybe his support group is afraid to tell him about past or impending indiscretions that will upset him. If that is the case, and he has no desire to know these things, then he is the incompetent, and he should fire himself.

In 2008, during Barack Obama's presidential campaign, Michelle Obama commented: "for the first time in my adult life I am proud of my country because it feels like hope is finally making a comeback". With Mr. Obama's 2014 national approval rating at an all time low in the high 30s, I wonder if Michelle is still proud of her country? More Americans disapprove of Mr. Obama's policies and the direction he is taking the country than approve of it. Kicking Obama while he is down may seem mean-spirited and racist but we are in a battle for the very existence of America as we know it. The only two completely truthful things Mr. Obama has said since starting his campaign in 2007 are: (paraphrasing) "I am going to fundamentally change the United States of America." "I am going to bankrupt the coal industry." In five short years he has almost completed both. If he continues on the same path at the current pace both statements will be absolutely accurate. He will be able to hang his own giant flag displaying "MISSION ACCOMPLISHED".

"The biggest problems that we're facing right now have to do with George Bush trying to bring more and more power into the executive branch and not go through Congress at all. And that's what I intend to reverse when I'm president of the United States." These words were spoken by Senator Barack Obama on March 31, 2008. Mr. Obama was lying when he made those statements but it is okay because now liberals contend that all politicians lie when they are campaigning. I have to assume he was talking about what George Bush did with executive orders. Mr. Obama is on track to produce more executive orders than George Bush did. Several of Mr. Obama's executive orders go way beyond his authority. So he lied about reversing the practice that he claimed Mr. Bush so abused. Mr. Obama has, throughout his entire presidency, made every effort to legislate on his own without allowing Congress to participate in any fashion. When Mr. Obama doesn't get his way he feels he has no recourse but to proceed on his own. He has continually, including very recently, threatened Congress with the statement: "I have a pen and a phone" meaning he will continue to do more constitutionally-challenged legislation. That is not how our Constitution was designed to work. There are three co-equal branches of government: executive, legislative, and judicial and each is the watchdog over the other two. No one in the other two branches of government wants to be called "racist" so accountability is flushed down the toilet. If Mr. Obama is the constitutional scholar and teacher that he has claimed to be, he would have to know what he is doing is completely above and beyond his authority. Don't take my word for that, the liberals very own constitutional guru Jonathan Turley will tell you exactly the same thing: Obama has "crossed the constitutional line" with his "go it alone" policies.

At this point, many are calling me a racist. So now I will give them an opportunity to call me a "birther". My interpretation/opinion of "natural-born citizen" and "naturalized-citizen" are starkly different. I am not a lawyer or constitutional scholar; this is just my opinion. To me a natural-born citizen is an individual who is born on American soil, including American consulates and American military bases, to two American parents. Of course a child born to two American parents on foreign soil is also a natural born-citizen. Being born while your parents are on vacation in France does not void your American citizenship. A naturalized-citizen is someone who has legally submitted to the citizenship requirements of the United States and takes the oath of allegiance regardless of their parental status. A man/woman couple of naturalized-citizens will then give birth to natural-born citizens. I believe the Founding Fathers set this up this way to prevent dual-citizens from possessing the office of the President of the United States thus ending loyalty to a previous country. The Pilgrim settlements in the northeastern states initiated the process of natural-born citizenship but because of the wide spread citizen allegiance to King George of England the Founding Fathers were smart enough to make dual-citizenship a nonstarter for pursuing the office of President.

It is now time to get to the birther label. Regardless of where in the world Mr. Obama was born he is not a natural-born citizen. He had an American mother and may very well have even been born in Hawaii. But by his admission, his father is Kenyon. Kenyons were British citizens under British rule and carrying British passports in 1961 when Mr. Obama was born. If you agree with my interpretation of natural-born citizen, Mr. Obama does not qualify to be President of the United States. And I'm going to take it a step further and disenfranchise Republicans with this statement: for the exact same reasons Obama is not qualified to be President of the United States neither are Bobby Jindal, Marco Rubio, or Ted Cruz. Jindal and Rubio were born in the United States but their parents were not American citizens at the time of their birth. Cruz was born in Canada to a Canadian father and American mother making him Canadian. He may have renounced his Canadian citizenship and pledged allegiance to the United States of America but now he is a naturalized-citizen, not natural-born. Any one of the three men would be an excellent president, but I will not vote for any of the three for Commander-in-Chief. I try not to be a hypocrite, unlike the liberals who extensively investigated what they considered to be John McCain's bogus citizenship even though he was born in Panama to American parents. Those same liberals made zero effort to investigate Mr. Obama's citizenship knowing at the time he had a Kenyon father. Go figure!

When Mr. Obama first came into office and was doing fiscally irresponsible things, I gave him the benefit of the doubt. I attributed his and his adviser's actions to a lack of economic knowledge. I believed there would be adults in the federal government that would bring him back onto the economically feasible track. As time went on and he continually used poor judgment I began to feel his actions were intentional. His fiscal irresponsibility has reached a level that is destroying the American economy. I believe Mr. Obama and his administration and liberals in general have determined that the only way for them to stay in power and control the American people is to first destroy the long-standing American way of life. The ideas of individualism and personal responsibility do not jibe with the liberal mindset of complete dependence on government. The policies currently coming out of the administration's back room negotiations and put into play by Mr. Obama's executive orders are no longer rooted in naïveté and ignorance. The bulk of the long-standing liberal playbook was written back in the 1960s but the roots of liberalism go back many years into American history. It has come off the shelf on occasion but it was waiting for the right leader to be in the position that allowed him/her to do as he/she pleased with no criticism allowed by the people in general and the Republican Party specifically. That leader has emerged in the form of Barack Obama as the first black president and is completely immune from criticism because of his race. It does not matter whether you are truly a racist or not, you are not allowed to criticize the president's policies and actions. The same will be true if Hillary Clinton campaigns for and wins the presidency in 2016. The only thing that will change is the name we will be called. We will still be racists; but we will be sexists as well.

This last thing will wrap up my racist rant and I will move on to another topic that will reveal some other part of my despicable personality. I have had my fill of hearing Obama brag about how he single-handedly killed Osama bin Laden. The incessant bragging can only have a detrimental effect on the way the world terrorists perceive America. Obama claims Osama's death and the continued killing of Al Qaeda leaders with drone strikes has Al Qaeda now being run by their junior varsity. If I were at any leadership level in Al Qaeda I would consider that the ultimate "triple dog dare". Based on the amount of terrorist activity around the world that is linked directly to Al Qaeda, I believe they took it the same way. I won't be surprised to see some very bold action by Al Qaeda in the near future. Let's hope that it won't be on American soil.

UPDATE: I didn't even finish this book before that prediction came true. The Islamic State in Iraq and Syria (ISIS), an Al Qaeda affiliate but more brutal, has retaken several of the larger Iraqi cities and has surrounded Baghdad. Baghdad may fall before this book is in print. The intent is to establish an Islamic caliphate in the entire region. A caliphate is a form of religious government that allows a supreme leader to control every aspect of muslim life using his interpretation of the Koran. The brutality and atrocities that are being forced on the Iraqi people by ISIS makes Saddam Hussein and his sons Uday and Qusay look like amateurs.

# OBAMACARE

*"Who needs enemies when you've got Republican Surrenderists for Obamacare waiting in the wings?"*
Michelle Malkin

No matter how many horror stories and bad reports we receive about Obamacare the liberals continue to dress up that ugly stepsister and push her off on us like she is our Saturday night dream date. They will do anything to salvage this long enough to get it converted to a single-payer system. And make no mistake, that has been the primary goal of this legislation from the beginning. Here's a House Minority Leader Nancy Pelosi (D – CA) quote talking about Obamacare: "We see it as an entrepreneurial bill, a bill that says to someone, if you want to be creative and be a musician or whatever, you can leave your work, focus on your talent, your skill, your passion, your aspirations because you will have health care." I've heard that people can't live on love alone but I didn't realize a person could quit their job and live on free health care alone. Senator Chuck Schumer (D – NY) had these brilliant words of wisdom for Obama care recipients: "What CBO (Congressional Budget Office) said is many American workers would have freedom. Now that's a good word. Freedom to do things that they couldn't do. The single mom who's raising three kids has to keep the job because of healthcare, can now spend some time raising those kids. That's a family value." This gets better and better, now even kids can live on health care alone. Senate Majority Leader Harry Reid (D – NV) has stated publicly that Obama care is just the first step toward abandoning the need for insurance and moving directly into single-payer healthcare. Obama's Treasury Secretary Jack Lew has a short memory: at a commencement address at Georgetown University Mr. Lew praised Obama and Congress for their ability to overcome partisanship to pass Obamacare. Jack was either intentionally deceptive or needs to schedule testing for dementia; Obamacare passed without a single Republican vote!

Remember in the early 90s when Obamacare was called Hillarycare? Those were the days when Republicans still had a strong spine. Republicans pointed out that it was complicated, expensive, and virtually impossible to implement so the liberals abandoned it. Hillarycare was soundly defeated before it even grew legs to run. Not so with Obamacare. The Republican warnings about Obamacare were completely ignored this time and in the dark of night, with some legislative shenanigans, and an absolutely one-sided liberal vote, Obamacare was hatched. Just so we are clear, let me explain why I am comparing this to Hillarycare: Obama and his socialist following were not smart enough to write this massive legislation in the short time frame from his election to Obamacare having been introduced. My belief is that Hillarycare was taken off the shelf next to her Rose Law firm billing records, dusted off, updated, and presented to the public as Obamacare. The 3,000 pages sat in a closet for 20 years just waiting for the opportunity to out itself. The tsunami that brought a hard-core, socialist president into office, that everyone was afraid to oppose, was the perfect time to spring the big surprise. It worked well because the only defense necessary to defend Obamacare and shut up the Republicans was to call them racists. It made a 50 year old socialist dream come true.

For at least two years before the 2012 presidential election Obama continually lied about the specifics of Obamacare to protect his candidacy; It was revealed in 2010 that Obama and his administration knew that the Affordable Care Act (ACA) would not allow Americans to keep their doctors or their current insurance policies. The implementation of Obamacare has proven both of those scenarios not to be true. As far back as 1994 when Obamacare was called Hillarycare, there was a memo from "TODD" to the Clintons that warned the Clintons "not to promise you can keep your doctor because we know it not to be true". Obama, his administration staff, and his reelection campaign staff had to know it was a 20-year-old lie. But the truth had to be withheld from the American public to prevent damage to his reelection. Another Obama lie that has been revealed is the promise that Obamacare would lower your health insurance costs by $2,500 per year. It was also promised that the ACA would give you access to better healthcare. The truth is the ACA has raised costs of healthcare and has severely limited access to many doctors and many of the best hospitals by eliminating them from the eligibility lists that are available to patients. I have to assume they were eliminated from eligibility because being the best might also compute to costing the most. Just keep in mind cheaper is very seldom better. You get what you pay for.

Does anyone in their right mind honestly believe that Obama's many extensions of healthcare mandates are actually being done to benefit the people? Obama started his CYA program before the 2012 presidential election to protect his candidacy, his private industry donors, and his union campaign donors. He is now safely in office. Now he has to protect the balance of his presidency and he is doing so by making illegal changes to Obamacare to protect his liberal cronies in the 2014 elections who in turn will protect him for the last two years of his presidency. If you couple his dismal approval ratings with the outrage of Obamacare fully implemented, Obama could easily lose the Senate in 2014. Even though the Senate and the House would both be in control of the Republicans they wouldn't have the spine to impeach Obama but impeachment has to be on his mind. Everyone, including the Republican speaker of the House, John Boehner, claims Obamacare is now the law of the land and we just can't do anything to change it. I would like to point out to Mr. Boehner that you have allowed Mr. Obama to change the United States Constitution on several occasions over the last five years without a peep from you. The Constitution has been the law of the land for 225 years! Explain yourself, please.

As the pressures continue to mount to save his signature legislation, his liberal friends in Washington, and his public sector donors, Mr. Obama has to continue to make illegal changes to the Obamacare laws that will affect the 2016 elections and beyond. He has to maintain enough liberals with enough power to protect Obamacare into the future. His hope is that regardless of how detrimental Obamacare is to Americans and the US economy it will be so firmly ensconced it will be impossible to eliminate. But regardless of the number of changes and delays he makes it has got to eventually kick-in in its entirety and begin to function on its own. I have no faith that Obamacare will ever function properly and I believe Obama and the socialist liberals believe the same thing. All this screaming, fighting, and name-calling are merely the foreplay to the climactic result of "single-payer" healthcare. That has been their goal for 50 years and their dream of Obamacare becoming single-payer will be realized in the next few years barring any legislative or judicial interference. Obamacare is designed to destroy every last possibility of the private insurance industry being able to recover or survive the changes being forced on it. Obamacare policies will become so bad that the liberals will claim they have no choice but to totally eliminate the evil private insurance industry and take over all aspects of American healthcare and provide it through the caring and benevolent government, which means taxpayers will take a giant financial hit but will have to accept lesser quality healthcare. Here's a partial list of the illegal delays Mr. Obama has made to Obamacare, the so-called "law of the land":

**July 2013** – one year delay for employers with more than 50 employees mandating them to provide insurance to all employees.

**November 2013** – one year extension to allow people to keep their old insurance plans in place.

**November 2013** – one year extension for small business health exchanges.

**February 2014** – one year extension from employee mandate with 50 to 100 employees.

**March 2014** – two-year extension from having to change to ACA compliance plans.

**March 2014** – extends enrollment deadline beyond the March 31 enrollment deadline for those who started the sign-up process prior to midnight on March 31, 2014.

If Obamacare truly is the "law of the land" how has Obama avoided consequences for arbitrarily picking parts of the law to enforce or delay with no authority to do so? Actually, I can answer my own question. The Republican establishment has no stomach or spine to confront Obama for fear of being called racists. The liberal establishment has no desire to confront Obama because they support what he is doing. They know as well as everyone else he has done what he has done in order to protect his majority in the Senate for his last two years in office.

There have been so many bad stories resulting from the implementation of Obamacare that it is becoming impossible to keep track of them all. Millions of Americans have lost their health care. Millions of Americans have lost their favorite doctors; not just primary care doctors but also their specialists. Millions of Americans premiums went up considerably. Millions of Americans co-pays went up considerably. Millions of Americans out of pocket expenses went up considerably. Thousands of doctors and thousands of hospitals are no longer available to the American public. Not only will there be a severe shortage of doctors resulting in a lack of quality care, there will also be a severe shortage of hospital beds available to patients. Thousands of doctors are closing their practices and hundreds of hospitals are closing their doors because of Obamacare. Even though Obama and the liberals claim none of this is happening you don't have to look very hard to find plenty of examples to dispute their claims. Senate Majority Leader Harry Reid doubled down on the lies by claiming all the stories brought forth by American citizens are bogus. The sad fact is there's more to come from Obamacare and a good portion of it will be even worse than what we are already experiencing.

There have been stories that Obamacare is even causing divorce. Couples are divorcing so they qualify for Obamacare premium subsidies because as a couple their income was too high to qualify. You sure can't dispute that logic! There is nothing good about federal laws and policies that force American taxpayers to have to do that sort of life change to survive the madness.

There are many cases that Obamacare has been responsible for temporary layoffs, outright firings, and the reason for no new hires. Employers can't afford the additional cost they will be hit with if they have a certain number of employees and they are required to provide health insurance for all. Employers are also cutting hours of full time employees to part-time to prevent having to provide insurance. Whether that is right or wrong on the employer's part is not my determination to make. But the employer should never have been put in a position to have to make those kinds of decisions. The cost of Obamacare can, and will, cause the closings of many small businesses. Wouldn't it be more prudent to have the jobs rather than mandated healthcare? The fact is, without the job there is no decent healthcare. I recall a story I read about a company that was going to have to terminate some employees to be able to afford to pay the mandated health costs of Obamacare. To determine which employees to terminate company management went into their employee parking lot and looked for Obama bumper stickers. The owners of those vehicles were the employees they terminated. That attaches a warm and fuzzy meaning to the term "poetic justice". I would like to commend the management of that company for the common sense approach they used to solve the problem.

I've read that health care accounts for 16% of the US economy. The truth is health care accounts for 100% control of the American people. Once the government can dictate your health and well-being they then have control of everything else in your life. If you don't do exactly as the government says they can punish you by limiting your access to health care. I see nothing in the government's past actions to prove they would do otherwise. The government will have the authority to determine what products or activities are unsafe or unhealthy and thus have the right to outlaw it. They will control all of what you eat and drink. All forms of tobacco and smoking, except for marijuana, will be outlawed. There will be no form of contact sports, publicly or privately. There will be no more outdoor recreational activities allowed. Everyone will drive the same size mini-car and larger freight vehicles will travel on their own taxpayer funded roads. You will be required to wear a specially designed head protection system at all times. When you reach a predetermined age you will automatically be denied further medical treatment regardless of your ability to pay for it on your own because that wouldn't be fair to those who don't have the ability to pay. Please keep in mind that those in political power that establish all of these policies, laws, and regulations will be personally exempted from all of them. Welcome to the future ruled by single-payer healthcare!

Liberals are claiming that Republicans have never come up with any suggestions for alternatives to Obamacare and that is simply a lie. Republicans continually tried to offer amendments to Obamacare but their amendments were never even considered by the liberals. The reason I know the liberals are lying is because here are a few of the common sense things that Republicans offered over the course of the Obamacare one-sided presentation:

**Portability:** once you have insurance you keep it for life; this instantly alleviates the problem of pre-existing conditions; eliminate state-to-state prohibitions.

**Tort Reform:** set limits on awards for medical malpractice cases thus lowering the costs of overall insurance premiums to the consumers; lessen the need for lawyers.

**Insurance Benefits:** establish specific dollar amounts for specific injury benefits and specific dollar amounts for death benefits thus eliminating confusion and again the need for lawyers.

**Competitive Purchasing:** let the market determine rates by allowing consumers to pick what coverage they want and how much they're willing to pay for it; half of the population would want coverage for prostate cancer but not maternity coverage; it would be exactly the opposite for the other half of the population; not requiring people to pay for coverage they don't want or need would lower the cost of premiums.

**Youth Policies:** allow young people to choose full coverage policies or catastrophic coverage only; this would alleviate the need to have children on their parent's policies until the age of 26.

Okay, so a couple of those are not completely Republican inventions, but I felt the need to include them in the list. If the insurance industry had most of the above things already in place, the industry and the American people would not now be suffering through the pains of Obamacare. It would've been smarter and cheaper for the American taxpayers to simply have paid the premiums to provide insurance for those Americans that didn't have it. But the liberal/socialist way of doing things is always the longest, hardest, and most expensive route to take to any destination.

# MAINSTREAM MEDIA

*"Our liberty depends on the freedom of the press and that cannot be limited without being lost."*
                                                                    Thomas Jefferson

It is called "MSM" for short. Some call it the "lame stream media". I have my own affectionate name for the media. I call it "CARTOONS" which stands for **C**ontrolling **A**nd **R**epeating **T**he **O**bama **O**nly **N**ews **S**ervice. If that doesn't make sense to you then change the word "controlling" to "creating". Is that better?

I have been watching national news since the late 60s. Even though the likes of Walter Cronkite, Tom Brokaw, Diane Sawyer, Harry Reasoner, Chet Huntley, David Brinkley, Peter Jennings, Bernard Shaw, and Howard K. Smith all leaned a little left you could still normally depend on the bulk of what they said to be true. Their left-of-center politics did not prevent them from reporting liberal scandals. Most of them still adhered to the basics of truthful journalism. They were the only source of news the American public had. They were the only government watchdogs the American public had. Even though they had the power to shape the news that Americans received, they still maintained their personal integrity. I intentionally left Dan Rather off the list because he gave in to his hard-core liberal ideology and allowed it to taint his integrity.

Anyway, all that integrity and truthful reporting began to change during the Bill Clinton presidency. Many of the mainstream television outlets became openly pro-liberal in order to protect their newly elected savior Bill Clinton. All the Clinton scandals were intentionally covered up, misreported, or underreported like his philandering, illegal campaign funds, perjury, release of military technology to the Chinese, pardoning crooks and felons, renting out the Lincoln bedroom, illicit sex in the Oval Office, threat of impeachment, the loss of his law license. By the way, that is a very small portion of the criminal activity that took place in the White House during Bill and Hillary Clinton's eight years.

With the introduction of 24/7 cable news networks that weren't all in Bill's pocket, a lot of the scandalous activities began to leak to the public. The liberals no longer had 100% control of what the public heard. That is also about the time that "shoot the messenger" and "hang the whistle-blower" mantras began. Without being able to defend against the volume of detrimental information, the liberals had to resort to destroying the people and the organizations that released the information. With the election of George Bush the MSM had to switch from defense to attack mode. The justification for the incessant nastiness toward Bush was to prevent him and his evil administration from doing irreparable damage to the MSM's sacred liberal domestic policies and their favorite foreign dictators.

Even though Bill Clinton is still a liberal icon, he is not held in the same high esteem as the current recipient of MSM idolatry, Barack Obama. In the nearly 50 years I've been watching news I have never witnessed anything that even remotely compares to the worship of Barack Obama by the MSM. Not even Clinton attained this level. Journalists have lowered themselves from being reporters of relevant news to being toadies that cover up relevant news. They've given up their right to be members of the honorable profession of journalism. Benjamin Franklin and the other Founding Fathers would not be proud.

The MSM not calling Obama to account for anything unconstitutional that he does is a complete disservice to the American people. They should be protecting the American people from Barack Obama, not the other way around. They are not holding him accountable and that allows him to be bolder and go even farther. This is exactly the same scenario that has unfolded around the world. Obama's weak foreign-policy has emboldened the world's bad guys and is allowing them to step out and do whatever they want knowing Obama is not going to hold them accountable either. That lack of accountability, both at the domestic level and the foreign level, is extremely dangerous.

Do you recall how the MSM hammered on Bush on a daily basis about the war deaths from Iraq and Afghanistan? They claimed it was extremely important to the American people to show the arriving coffins. The daily death count watch ended the second Obama entered office. It all went silent. All that could be heard were the crickets. The MSM war critics were nowhere to be found. The Afghan fighting under Bush accounted for 575 American hero deaths in 88 months. To date, the death toll linked to Obama is in excess of 1,600 in 51 months. Obama withdrew from Iraq and stopped the American death toll, thank you Mr. Obama. But everything that America sacrificed in Iraq was for naught because Al Qaeda has already regained control of several Iraqi cities. Mr. Obama promised to end both of those conflicts as soon as he got into office. He did remove the American presence from Iraq but maybe prematurely. For whatever reason, Mr. Obama has always considered Afghanistan to be the more noble war and obviously still feels the same way because he intends to leave between

6,000 and 20,000 soldiers in Afghanistan through 2024. It doesn't seem like enough troops to do much of anything other than give target practice to the Taliban.

Another Obama campaign promise that never came true was the closing of the Guantánamo Bay terrorist detention center. The constant MSM harping on the imaginary suffering of the scum that inhabited that prison during the Bush years has gone silent. Nothing has changed at the prison. The guards are the same, the food is the same, and all of the living conditions are identical. The only thing that changed is the Commander-In-Chief. Ladies and gentlemen of the MSM, you embarrass yourselves.

The CARTOONS have given Obama cover for every scandal that has happened during his administration, and as you well know there's plenty of it to cover. The MSM is a laughingstock and a detriment to the American people but it doesn't realize it, or more accurately, doesn't care. The MSM created the legend and the myth that is Obama, and now they won't bring him down from the pedestal for fear their ignorance will be exposed. Too late people, your lip-lock on Barack's butt-cheek is out in the open for all to see. Bill Clinton still has a giant hickey on his posterior from his years in the presidency.

If the American people want the truth they have to go to the Internet or the cable news networks who don't worship the very ground that Obama walks on. One of the best sources of accurate and impartial news is the Drudge Report. Liberals hate it for that reason. They claim it is wholly a Republican stronghold. That could not be further from the truth. Drudge features information and articles from sources totally independent of Drudge Report. Drudge does not show favoritism. It is equally as likely to find a report detrimental to a Republican or a Republican action or policy as it is to find the same damaging information about a liberal or a liberal policy. Even Fox News premieres liberal commentators in many of their shows allowing the liberal point of view to rear its ugly head even in a quasi-conservative atmosphere. As far as honest and accurate reporting goes, UK Daily Mail is a better source for American news than the American MSM.

# HILLARY

This will be the scariest chapter in the entire book. The scariest thing I can say: Hillary Clinton may be our next president. If that doesn't make you want to hide under the bed then you're not afraid of anything. I cannot imagine anything scarier than that, with the exception of what is going to happen to America for the next two and half years under Obama. Given the chance, twice, Americans elected a completely unqualified and dangerous socialist because of his skin color. Those same people will try to elect, twice, a completely unqualified and dangerous socialist because of her gender. Neither of those scenarios speak well of the American left but the fact remains abundantly clear: Hillary Clinton could be the next American president just because she is a woman!

It seems none of Hillary's supporters can come up with a single thing she achieved during her four years as US Secretary of State. Being the generous and compassionate man that I am I'm going to help them out:

1. The Arab/Israeli conflict has turned in the Arabs favor because of Hillary's lack of enthusiasm for the plight of Israelis who are supposed to be our allies.

2. The Muslim brotherhood is in Egypt, Libya, and Syria.

3. Putin has renewed his efforts to reinstate the old USSR. I guess that reset button you offered Russia is working after all, Hillary.

4. Al Qaeda was retaking the Middle East a piece at a time under Hillary's watch.

5. Iraq military is now buying supplies from their former enemy Iran.

6. Iran's nuke program is on the verge of being realized.

7. North Korea restarted one of its nuclear reactors.

8. China is threatening Japan and several other neighbors.

9. Pakistani government is negotiating with Al Qaeda and the Taliban.

Even though there are several more equally relevant achievements, I don't want to give the Hillary supporters too much help before she even announces her candidacy. To be fair, I should mention that she achieved all the above with the help of Barack Obama. "Spread the credit", so to speak.

That's enough of the good stuff; let's discuss something else that happened under Hillary's watchful eye. The most noteworthy was the

Benghazi, Libya terrorist attack on our US consulate buildings, the US Ambassador, and support personnel on September 11, 2012. The attack itself was horrendous but Hillary's indignant response during questioning in Congress was equally disgusting. During the questioning Hillary snapped and in a loud nasty tone said this to Congress: "With all due respect, the fact is, we had four dead Americans! Was it because of a protest or was it because of guys out for a walk one night who decided they'd go kill some Americans? What difference at this point does it make? It is our job to figure out what happened and do everything we can to prevent it from ever happening again". I'll talk slowly, Hillary, in the hopes that you can understand the answer to your question: The difference it makes is to the four dead Americans and their grieving families. Your righteous indignation makes me sick to my stomach. The difference it makes is embodied in the last sentence of your statement. If you honestly feel that we need to figure out what happened to prevent it from happening again, why are you so snarky and uncooperative when that is exactly what Congress is trying to do. You are in CYA mode with four dead American heroes in an effort to salvage your own future political aspirations. There are many reasons to prevent Hillary from being a future Commander-In-Chief but this alone should disqualify her. The primary job of the President of the United States is to keep Americans safe. Obama and Hillary have failed miserably. On the other hand, lack of achievements or qualifications shouldn't stop Hillary's bid for the White House, it didn't stop Obama.

In Miami, February 2014, Hillary Clinton made the following statement: "Ultimately, having access to health insurance not connected to employment, subsidized, as it is under the ACA (Obamacare), liberates you to choose what to do in your life. You don't have to take a job, as so many in my generation did, just to have health insurance". This statement is so wrong in so many ways I'm not sure where to start. First of all, she states that having insurance connected to having a job is bad, but having insurance paid for by taxpayers and controlled by the government is good. Secondly, this is a woman who salivates at the thought of being our next president. For her to encourage people to quit their jobs and let others take care of them is utterly irresponsible. Lastly, for her to infer that the American people of her generation, baby boomers, only sought employment in order to have health insurance is an insult to the offspring of the greatest generation; the generation that fought and died to give their children the opportunity to have a decent job. Hillary's statement is indicative of the very thought process that comes from her circle of friends who were hippies and socialists growing up and are now tenured socialist college professors all across our great nation. Just say "NO" to Hillary in 2016. There, I've done it, my latest jump into the sexist cesspool. I feel refreshed.

Just a couple more tidbits about Hillary then I will leave her alone.

Hillary refused to put Boca Haram on the active terrorist watch-list when she was Secretary of State. Boca Haram is a Nigerian Islamic terrorist organization with Al Qaeda ties. They are the terrorists that recently kidnapped 300 Nigerian Christian girls and are using them to extort ransom money; sell into slavery; or keep as teenage brides. The first-order of business after the kidnapping was to force the girls to convert to Islam or die. Had they been on the terrorist watch-list maybe people would have been a little more diligent in following their actions. So much for a liberal watching out for the children.

Because of the extent of what Hillary called the "bimbo eruptions", a result of Bill's philandering, she has had to wage a more profound war on women than what the Republicans are being accused of.

The US State Department misplaced, lost, or stole $6 billion of taxpayer money during the tenure of Hillary Clinton. That represents approximately 10% of the State Department's annual budget. So now we have to scratch "diligent fiscal manager" off Hillary's qualification list. I couldn't find it to scratch it off; it must be on a different page of qualifications.

Many liberals questioned the ability of Ronald Reagan, Bob Dole, and John McCain to be president because of their elevated ages. I guess Hillary's age can be a campaign issue because when she runs in 2016 she will be at about the same age each of them were when they ran for president.

And last, but certainly not least, is Hillary's health: Did the concussion help or hurt her cognitive thinking process? Did it take one month of recovery as Hillary's doctor said or did it take six months of recovery like Bill said? A six month recovery time would definitely indicate a more serious injury than a one month recovery time. On the other hand, a good knock on the head might be just what the doctor ordered to shake loose a little common sense from an intolerant liberal noggin!

# TREASON *and* SEDITION

*"A nation can survive its fools, even the ambitious. But it cannot survive treason from within...for the traitor appears not to be a traitor...he rots the soul of a nation...he infects the body politic so that it can no longer resist."*

Marcus Tullius Cicero

The Sedition Act of 1918 was an extension of the act originally produced in 1917. Keep in mind World War I was just wrapping up when they made the amendments in 1918. The Act would not allow the use of "disloyal, profane, scurrilous, or abusive language about the United States government, its flag, or its Armed Forces". It was repealed in 1920, which is too bad, because we could prosecute every current liberal/socialist in the US. But in keeping with the theme of this book I would be remiss if I left out mentioning the sedition by many establishment Republicans. Since the act has been repealed I won't go into it further other than to mention we are currently in a war against terrorism and maybe something of that sort could be reinstated. But, it pretty much flies in the face of the free speech outlined in Amendment 1 of the Constitution of the United States.

Section 3 of the United States Constitution defines treason with basically two criteria. The first criteria states an American citizen commits treason if he bands with other American citizens to wage war against the US. The second criterion states that it is treasonous to give aid and comfort to America's enemies.

This is the chapter that is going to get me a review by the Secret Service that will make the IRS audit I've earned pale in comparison. I should notify my family and friends about what they can expect. I am not going to go very far into the past. I will limit my perception of treason or treasonous acts to those public figures I am familiar with. I apologize if you are feeling treasonous and I left you off the list but I am dealing with limited space in this book. Here's my list:

1. **John Kerry:** in Paris in 1970, John Kerry met with representatives of the Communist North Vietnamese government. It was illegal for an American citizen to meet and attempt to negotiate with a foreign country. In April 1971 John Kerry testified before the U.S. Congress that American soldiers had systematically terrorized and murdered Vietnamese civilians. He was acting as a spokesman for Vietnam

Veterans Against the War. With no evidence in hand he was allowed to portray our American warriors as war criminals. John Kerry teamed up with the antiwar radicals in order to ingratiate himself to the American liberal base for purely personal reasons. His motive was to garner support for a future political career. It worked very well for him. Mr. Kerry, with his less than stellar Vietnam service, has no moral authority to judge the veterans who served honorably in that war. His accusations are especially egregious when you consider that more than 58,000 young American boys lost their lives in that faraway jungle. In no way does his Vietnam service qualify him to have been a United States Senator. Even worse, as the US Secretary of State, he is the face of America around the world. Kerry just recently lowered himself to a new depth that even I didn't believe he could achieve. He assured the American people that the 5 most despicable and dangerous Taliban leaders released from Guantanamo Bay prison won't be able to harm Americans. I'm not even sure how he said that and kept a straight face while saying it. On top of that he was able to defend Bowe Bergdahl who was released from his Taliban cohorts in exchange for the five terrorists. Bergdahl had already been labeled a traitor by his compatriots.

2. **Jane Fonda:** Ms. Fonda posted not long ago that she ached for elephants and monkeys and monarch butterflies. But, as "Hanoi Jane", there is not one ounce of compassion in her for the military serviceman and their families that she disrespected and endangered during the Vietnam War. When most American celebrities were going to South Vietnam to entertain American troops Jane was on a propaganda tour for the North Vietnamese communists. She cries over how little time she has left personally but never shed a tear over the American pilots that were shot down by the antiaircraft gun she so jubilantly sat on in Hanoi in 1972. Many of those pilots ran out of time in the early 70s, Jane, and didn't make it to the ripe old age of 76 as you have. If they survived, they may have spent many years in the "Hanoi Hilton", not the type of accommodations you would choose for yourself. Jane waited 28 years to apologize for her actions of 1972. In 2000 Jane Fonda made an apology based on liberal ideology which means she didn't apologize for what she did but basically was sorry that it created such a hatred of her personally. Sorry doesn't cut it Jane. Some things are just unforgivable. There is one last thing to keep in mind about the ideology of Jane Fonda. She has lived a very successfully life under the protective umbrella of American capitalism. But she is as anti-American today as

when she made the following comment to students at the University of Michigan in November 1970: "If you understand what communism was, you would hope, you would pray on your knees that we would someday become communist". Someone that radical does not change with age.

3. **Bill Clinton:** In the late 1990s Bill allowed American military technology to be sold to the Communist Chinese for campaign cash. If you doubt that statement, research the names Bernard Schwartz, Charlie Trie, John Huang, and Johnny Chung. Bill Clinton allowed Loral Space and Communications and Hughes Electronics to sell military secrets such as rocket improvements and targeting technology for ICBMs (Intercontinental Ballistic Missile). I recall at the time the Chinese missile targeting was "hit or miss", but mostly miss. On a good day they could put an ICBM within 100 miles of its intended target. With Mr. Clinton's help, they can now put an ICBM into a 55 gallon drum from thousands of miles away. If you think that Bill's wife Hillary won't sell her soul for campaign cash, you need to reevaluate your thinking.

4. **Lynne Stewart:** Ms. Stewart was counsel for Omar Abdel-Rahman the mastermind of the 1993 World Trade Center bombing. She was convicted of perjury for lying about giving messages from Abdel-Rahman to his American-killing Al Qaeda related terrorist group. She was sentenced to 10 years but was released after only three because she contracted breast cancer. Another example of how dangerous the "bleeding heart liberal" ideology is to the United States of America. In liberal circles, traitors such as her become heroes. After all, that bomb in the basement of the World Trade Center was only "workplace violence".

5. **Ed Snowden:** At what point does a whistleblower become a traitor or a traitor become a whistle-blower? The way I see it Ed gave up any hope of getting whistle-blower status the second he fled the country and threatened the United States with additional security leaks. The title "traitor" was tattooed on his forehead the second he accepted asylum in Russia. I find it appalling that any American would consider Mr. Snowden a whistle-blower after having taken millions of American national security memos to Communist Russia. Mr. Snowden can claim that he has no intentions of giving up specific American secrets to Russia but I'd be willing to bet that Vladimir Putin doesn't feel the same way. I don't think Mr. Snowden has the fortitude to resist the

KGB if they decide to obtain information from him. The KGB will not start with something as simple as water boarding. A few years in a Russian gulag may make Mr. Ed begin to feel a little homesick regardless how awful America is to him! One more quick question: What idiot in Washington would approve top secret clearance for someone of Snowden's background and age?

6. **Bill Ayers and Bernadine Dorn:** These two individuals were domestic terrorists in the US in the 1960s. They bombed the Pentagon. Another of their actions resulted in the death of a police officer. They escaped prosecution only because of some shoddy investigative work. Not long ago unrepentant Bill Ayers commented he didn't feel they had done enough destruction or created enough chaos to help their cause. These two stellar individuals are college professors in Chicago. But they're only a drop in the bucket; thousands of people just like them are teaching your children at the college level.

7. **Barack Obama:** The worst thing an American can do is go overseas or to the United Nations and badmouth the United States of America. It is especially wrong when the President of the United States does it. Mr. Obama's first order of business after becoming president was to go around the world and apologize for America being so domineering and hostile to the rest of the world. I was personally offended by his around the world "apology tour". The top reason Mr. Obama made this list is because of his total disregard for his oath of office: "I do solemnly swear that I will faithfully execute the Office of President of the United States, and will to the best of my ability, preserve, protect and defend the Constitution of the United States". Mr. Obama has from the very beginning of his administration completely disregarded the American Constitution. For him to have been a constitutional scholar he seems to have little understanding of its meanings. He disregards laws when he personally feels that they are unjust. He makes up his own rules with executive orders that fly in the face of the laws legally established by Congress. The worst part is the fact that both houses of Congress are as guilty as he is based on their indifference to what he is doing. His lack of a coherent foreign-policy has made the rest of the world unstable and dangerous, especially for Americans. He broke the law by releasing five Guantánamo Bay Taliban terrorists without so much as a mention to Congress who are required by law to receive 30 days notice before he releases anyone. If you had any doubt about Mr. Obama's treasonous intentions this should alleviate those doubts for good. His Obamacare

law will result in a quick, complete, and lasting destruction of the middle class in the United States. His domestic policies are intentionally destroying the economy. The nature of that intentional destruction is without question treasonous. It will establish only two permanent classes: the haves and have-nots; or put more bluntly, the government and the poor. He does not believe in American Exceptionalism and is doing everything in his power to turn us into a Third World country. Phil Robertson of Duck Dynasty fame recently said something to the effect: "We are a superpower being run by a Third World government". That is a pretty astute statement coming from the ignorant southern redneck that he is portrayed to be by the Christian-hating liberals.

8. **Chuck Hagel:** Secretary of Defense Hagel said that America is no longer the dominant force in the world arena and that we Americans need to get used to that fact. He is doing Mr. Obama's bidding by gutting the US military to pre-World War II levels because they claim we are in a postwar environment. I guess that means that we won't ever have any future need for the American military to be in a state of readiness. Hooray for this current administration for they have successfully ended all conflict around the world. I've always suspected Hagel was a RINO when he was a sitting senator. It turns out he was even worse than that by virtue of having accepted this appointment by Obama for Secretary of Defense. He has now allowed Obama the argument that even his Republican Secretary of Defense agrees we need to cut the military budget. Chuck, have you ever heard the term "useful idiot"? A treasonous act has been committed solely on the fact that an American military at pre-World War II levels will be stripped of the ability to keep American citizens safe and protect our interests in an increasingly hostile world. Keeping Americans safe is the responsibility of the American government; not protecting them is a treasonous violation of the US Constitution. Accepting and defending Mr. Obama's illegal and treasonous act of releasing the five Guantánamo Bay Taliban terrorists makes Mr. Hagel an accomplice to treason and therefore a traitor himself. Mr. Hagel lied when he remarked that they made the trade for the Taliban leaders for deserter Bowe Bergdahl to save his life. I saw Bergdahl walk to the helicopter from the Taliban vehicle and he didn't appear to be too much worse for wear. But even if he was bruised and scarred underneath his Taliban garb, he did not appear to be deathly ill as he was made out to be. On the same topic, Obama and Hagel have saved the life of that American military deserter and

have left an American hero to rot in a Mexican jail over a bogus gun charge. That is another example of liberal backwards thinking: save the criminal but disrespect the hero. Sgt. Andrew Tahmooressi has been locked up in a Tijuana jail for well over five months with no release date even mentioned. Sgt. Tahmooressi could be released with a phone call from Obama to the Mexican president. Mr. Hagel, you along with your President, are a disgrace to the American people.

All eight are legitimately on this list based on the second criterion that says it is treasonous to give aid and comfort to the enemy.

*"Impeachment should be reserved for treason, bribery, and high crimes and misdemeanors where the president's actions are great and dangerous offenses or attempts to subvert the Constitution and the most extensive injustice."*

George Mason

# NASA

*"Exploration is the essence of the human spirit. As evidenced by Jamestown's stature as the first permanent English settlement in America and NASA's missions beyond this world, the drive to explore the unknown has been one of the constants in the history of the nation."*
      Lesa Roe

The National Aeronautics and Space Administration came into existence in 1958 under President Dwight D. Eisenhower with the sole purpose in mind to compete against Russia for dominance in outer space. Russia beat us in nearly all categories of space flight except the United States astronauts landed on the moon in 1969 and managed to come home safely. There's been a lot of money spent by the United States taxpayers on manned space flights but space exploration has brought us many things in return. Tang, the original powdered orange drink, was developed for space as were such things as freeze-dried meals, memory foam, space blankets, Corning Ware, and did I mention Tang the original powdered orange drink?

The International Space Station (ISS) was developed and jointly owned by the United States, Russia, and 13 other countries. It provided American, Russian, and the other nation's astronauts a place to stay and do research rather than just float around in space staring at the stars. The United States initiated its space shuttle program in order to transport astronauts and equipment back and forth between Earth and ISS. Six different American shuttles completed 135 flights in a 30 year span beginning in 1981 and ending with Obama terminating the program in 2011. The total cost for 30 years of NASA programs was $196 billion and the lives of 14 astronauts. I should point out that American astronauts died on the earlier Apollo missions as well. They paved the way for the shuttle missions. Those were some very sad days in the long and stellar careers of our space pioneers.

The American shuttles were for 30 years the only space flights carrying humans. Since Obama retired all the shuttles the Russians have been transporting all humans on their craft. I could find no indication that the United States charged Russia for shuttling their astronauts and equipment but I did find that the Russians are charging the US $70 million per person per trip. Now because of the wimpy sanctions Obama has put on Russia for the invasion of Crimea and Ukraine the Russians are refusing to carry US astronauts at all. Since approximately half of ISS is American-owned

I recommend we send Lizard Lick Towing up on Branson's new Virgin Galactic spacecraft, cut our half off, bring it home and sell it for scrap. We could recoup some of the billions we spent on that program.

NASA is actively pursuing a mission to develop a system of capturing asteroids that are on a collision course with Earth. That program like all taxpayer-funded programs preceding it will be astronomically expensive (pun intended) but if it works it could literally save the planet. The best part about this program is Bruce Willis in the movie "Armageddon" has already shown NASA how to intercept and destroy a very large earthbound asteroid. All they have to do is load the necessary equipment, which has already been inventoried by Bruce, onto a rocket ship and have astronauts standing by to fly on short notice. I expect Obama will soon be receiving "thank you" notes from all the dictators around the world thanking him in advance for saving their pathetic lives. Once again American blood, sweat, and treasure will save the planet. This program may seem like "pie in the sky" (Sorry I couldn't help myself.), but at least it has a noble purpose as opposed to the NASA mission in the following paragraph.

According to NASA Administrator Charles Bolden NASA's new mission is to reach out to Muslim nations and teach them to appreciate their contributions to science. When I first heard this I thought it was a joke but I soon realized it was another way for Obama to mainstream Muslims into every day American life. This new program will be called "Hug-a-Muslim" and the program slogan will be: "Have you hugged your Muslim today?" Obama will soon initiate a national contest to establish what day of the year this new Muslim holiday will fall on. It will be a federal paid holiday and the post office and all other federal buildings will be closed that day. I want to get my picks in early so no one else will steal my ideas so I suggest it be celebrated on either Easter or the fifth day of Hanukkah or both just to cover all bases. That would allow Muslims, Christians, and Hebrews to celebrate their holidays all at the same time. Can you envision the camaraderie that would be taking place with all three of those holidays celebrated on the same day? It brings a tear to my eye just to think of it.

# DID YOU KNOW?

If you would like to read the full texts of the Declaration of Independence, the U.S. Constitution and the US Bill of Rights go to www.archives.gov. You will also find very good analysis about who produced our sacred federal documents and the motivation and processes that were involved in the production of them.

- It costs $228,000 per hour to fly Air Force One.

- If you are curious about virtually anything concerning our national debt go to www.treasurydirect.gov/govt/reports.

- Representative Nancy Pelosi was washing the feet of immigrants around Easter 2014. I believe she hoped the feet would be more sanitary when she kissed them. I believe maybe she should be washing a little higher up for the same reason. Pucker up Nancy.

- Feminist Amanda Marcotte said babies are "time-sucking monsters". That same thing could be said of you Amanda. It might also be said you are a waste of fresh air. You think Amanda is pro-abortion? Where do these people come from?

- An Obama/Biden donor received $20 million from the US taxpayers via a federal program called Overseas Private Investment Corporation to start up a Porsche dealership in Ukraine. The dealership is about to be owned by Vladimir Putin and Russia.

- Obama announced he will issue an executive order requiring schools to provide education to illegal children. He is going around Congress again to reinstate the Dream Act.

- There is a company called BioGenicFutures that has developed a spray that can remove your DNA wherever you leave it. Mr. Obama must be their best customer because he has been removing his fingerprints from all Washington scandals since the beginning of his administration.

- *"Anyone who doesn't regret the passing of the Soviet Union has no heart. Anyone who wants it restored has no brains."* That statement was made by Vladimir Putin. With the invasion of the Crimea and Ukraine methinks Mr. Putin has changed his mind.

- Pi Beta Phi sorority has been sponsoring all-you-can-eat taco fund-raisers all around the country in behalf of charities. Latino students at Harvard and Dartmouth are offended. I don't even know how to comment on that.

- The Obamacare exchanges in Maryland, Massachusetts, Oregon, and Nevada have spent $474 million and the exchanges still don't work.

- John Boehner, Republican Speaker of the House passed a vote to hold Lois Lerner, head of the IRS during their recent scandals, in contempt of Congress but indicated that he won't have her arrested. What was the purpose of the contempt charge?

- In 2013, Obama had 36,000 immigrants released from Immigration and Customs Enforcement (ICE) custody on to the streets of the United States. They committed crimes ranging from drunk driving to murder and treason. These weren't criminals awaiting trial; these were criminals that had already been convicted of their respective crimes.

- Liberals are claiming that the attacks on the American consulate buildings in Benghazi, Libya are no worse crimes than Nixon's Watergate scandal. If those two incidents are comparable shouldn't impeachment proceedings begin against Obama and have him resign like Nixon did? No one got so much as a paper cut during the Watergate break-ins. Four Americans died in Benghazi.

- The Veterans Administration spent $500 million on office remodels, furniture, and raises for the agency staff while our vets were dying on a waiting list. All I have to say is: "Shame on each and every one of you responsible for that disgusting situation".

- 4.5 million Americans were bitten by dogs in 2013; including 2 million children.

- Phyllis Schlafly's syndicated column Eagle Forum claims immigrants overwhelmingly support Democrats and big government.

- Obama finally admitted that passing amnesty for illegal immigrants will be better for Democrats than Republicans. Who would have thunk it?

- According to the White House Office of Management and Budget the number of federal employees has grown by 123,000 under Mr. Obama. Private sector jobs remain down by 1.1 million from the start of 2009 when Obama took office.

- The first black slave owner in the American colonies was a black man himself. Anthony Johnson was a "free Negro" who owned a 250 acre farm. His first permanent Negro slave was named John Casor. That puts a new twist on the American slavery story.

- Hillary Clinton was on the Board of Directors of that evil and racist retailer Walmart in the 1980s.

- There are nine public college presidents whose salaries exceed $1 million per year.

- There are 11 million Americans on disability.

- Gasoline prices have stayed above three dollars per gallon for over 3 ½ years straight.

- IRS employees owe in excess of $3.3 billion in back taxes.

- If we are going to continue to allow the British to invade America please let it be more Stuart Varneys and fewer Piers Morgans.

- If Congress spent less time talking about dope in professional sports they would have more time to talk about the dopes in their midst.

- The Federal Transportation Security Administration (TSA) in charge of airline passenger and luggage inspections does not need to spend billions on body-scanning equipment. They could issue each of their agents x-ray vision glasses that are available all over the Internet for less than $10 a pair. I hope I get some kind of finder's fee for helping out.

- An Environmental Protection Agency employee got caught watching porn sites at work for six hours per day for two and half years. That's over 5,000 hours of porn watching. At a salary of $120,000 per year he has cost the American taxpayer in excess of $300,000 plus benefits. This gives a whole new meaning to the Obama stimulus package. I wonder if his job is the one that was saved.

- The US taxpayers own 302,000,000 acres of US land including 118,000,000 acres of forest. I think that's enough. By the way, there is a large portion of that acreage that the taxpayers are not allowed to set foot on.

- The White House leaked the name of an active CIA operative on a trip to Kabul. It was inadvertent and there will be no consequences. When Scooter Libby mentioned the name of an inactive CIA operative he went to prison.

- The New York Times must have existed in the Thomas Jefferson era because he said this: *"Advertisements contain the only truths to be relied on in the newspaper."*

- Michelle Obama said that even with her Ivy League education she didn't know how to feed her kids; having said that, why does she feel qualified to tell us how to feed ours?

- The US patent office canceled six trademark registrations of the Washington Redskins football team. What legal authority are the unelected morons in the patent office using as a basis for destroying the property rights of the Redskins owners?

- Thomas Jefferson made a statement 200+ years ago concerning "Buy American": *"I have come to a resolution myself as I hope every good citizen will, never again to purchase any article of foreign manufacture which can be had of American make, be the difference of price what it may."* I/we should practice that very concept of "Buy American".

- Slate Magazine has claimed that a major drought in Syria, caused by global warming, is the reason the citizens of Syria erupted in revolt a couple years ago. The Syrian people obviously had never tired of being starved and murdered by their dictator Assad but they woke up when their deserts experienced a drought caused by global warming.

- There are 261 millionaires in the US Congress, 7 of the top 10 are Democrats.

- I'm going to end this chapter with some population predictions made by the US Census Bureau:

- US white population will increase by 12% by 2025 and 32% by 2050.

- US black population will increase by 17% by 2025 and 43% by 2050.

- US Asian population will increase by 32% by 2025 and 139% by 2050.

- US Hispanic population will increase by 52% by 2025 and 167% by 2050.

- If the above numbers are even close to correct, the Democrats don't need amnesty to have enough new voters to take over the US unless they are so impatient that they can't wait to birth them into existence.

# CONCLUSION

*"The only purpose of government is to protect the people."*  Thomas Jefferson

*"Government has laid its hands on health, housing, farming, industry, commerce, education, and to an ever increasing degree interferes with the people's right to know. Government tends to grow, government programs take on weights and momentum as public servants say, always with the best intentions. But the truth is that outside of its legitimate function, government does nothing as well or economically as the private sector of the economy."*  Ronald Reagan

Well, you're almost done. I sincerely hope you had as much fun reading this as I did writing it. When I first considered starting this project I wasn't sure I could expand on my narrow-minded opinions to the extent that I could actually author a book of any size. When I started making a list of chapter topics I had no idea there would end up being in excess of 50. I kept a notebook handy and whenever a topic or a specific fact popped into my head I would write it down. I told my wife that if I could fill the spiral notebook with my thoughts then I would, at that point, consider going ahead with a book. I did not realize at the time that I was so opinionated! This whole book idea came about because my wife got tired of me yelling at the cable news channels on TV. She seemed to feel I should share my opinions with the rest of humanity rather than torture her exclusively.

I jumped around a lot from topic to topic. I may have even used the same facts in different chapters. I may have been able to consolidate some chapters but it seemed more appropriate to make each of the topics an issue in and of itself. I may have allotted extra print to some specific topics but I still only scratched the surface compared to the extent that I could have gone. Some topics appropriately deserve additional scrutiny.

At any rate, I will continue my love of God, America, family, football, and apple pie. God bless you readers and God bless America!

www.ingramcontent.com/pod-product-compliance
Lightning Source LLC
Chambersburg PA
CBHW060251290526
45789CB00001B/286